The End of Time and the Beginning of Eternity

C. G. Deveaux

WestBow
PRESS
A DIVISION OF THOMAS NELSON

WestBow Press books may be ordered through booksellers or by contacting:

WestBow Press
A Division of Thomas Nelson
1663 Liberty Drive
Bloomington, IN 47403
www.westbowpress.com
1 (866) 928-1240

ISBN: 978-1-4908-0905-2 (sc)
ISBN: 978-1-4908-0906-9 (e)

Library of Congress Control Number: 2013916954

Printed in the United States of America.

WestBow Press rev. date: 10/31/2013

Dedication

I dedicate this book to the Father, Son, and Holy Spirit.
Without God, nothing is possible.

Contents

Preface

This book is about the meaning of life and the end times in which we are now living. It recounts my search for truth and is my personal testimony to the reader, written with the hope that I can share some truth and inspiration. Receiving Jesus as my Savior and Lord has been my greatest accomplishment in life. I ask the reader to keep an open heart and mind.

This book is also a warning of coming destruction to the world as we know it, a warning that hell is real. The good news is that, with Jesus as our Lord and Savior, we can be forgiven. Because of Jesus, we can live with the Father, Son, and Holy Spirit for eternity.

The end of time itself is drawing to a close. My greatest hope is that through this book the reader will get to know our Lord Jesus and learn some truth about Him. Jesus is the only way to heaven. Hell is real, and it is eternal. If my book can save one soul from eternal torment, the effort to write it will have been worth it.

After God showed me the truth, I sold one of my houses, quit my job, and began to study full-time from the Bible and scientific research. I have studied to be a minister and have built my own church. Now I have written this book. All this I have done for the glory of God and to help my fellow brothers and sisters find the truth.

May God bless the reader of this book.

Chapter 1

Searching for Truth

I was brought up in a Christian family, but my parents were not Christian. My grandmother was Christian and was involved with the church. My grandparents on my dad's side were Christian, but they didn't talk about it often. As a child I was raised in Toronto, Ontario, in Canada.

We lived in a haunted house on Pickering Street. I was too young to recall the encounters, but my parents and grandparents have stories to tell. I had to be moved out of my room because it was unnaturally cold and I had nightmares there. One time a boiling pot of water fell off the stove by itself. My parents witnessed bobby pins falling out of midair. My dad, being calm and cool, claimed, "As long as it's not dropping bricks, we will be okay." My mother reported that she was drying her hair when a table started moving on its own. My grandmother would not go upstairs one day, because she felt an evil presence.

There was another haunted house in my childhood—an old, spooky house in New Brunswick. It was already furnished with very old furniture, and the bedrooms were in the attic. My parents were staying there with my aunt and uncle, when they heard noises in the night. Each couple thought the noises were made by the others, but in the morning, they all confirmed that no one had gotten up.

In the same house, I had the worst nightmare of my life. I was about ten years old. In my dream, a force tried to possess me. At about four a.m., I woke up crying and then woke the whole family—and we stayed up. I told my mother what had happened in the dream, and she was astonished because she'd had the same dream.

My wife has been a witness to many miracles that have happened to me. She has also been inappropriately touched by a demonic presence. After that, we left the house and went to the lake. That seemed to work.

My family disregards all of these strange occurrences of the unknown. They don't seem to care or think much about it. So I took it upon myself to dig for the truth of what life was all about. I was in my late teens when I read the Bible and many other books about Buddhism and various religions, but I didn't find a clear answer.

I experimented with drugs, with an open mind to the spiritual realm. One night we had a party and indulged in drugs. I would like to point out that drugs may help one see the supernatural, but I would not recommend it. I think it is a shortcut, and nothing beats prayer and fasting as a proper way to seek God.

One guest was into the occult, and he told us strange stories. I personally didn't like him for his dark, occult side. As we enjoyed the night, he went to the washroom. He was gone a long time, so I went to check on him. As I went into the room, I saw that he was in distress. It was like he was being choked to death. I quickly broke the spell (demon) that had him. When we returned to the kitchen, he was so grateful. He blindfolded himself and offered himself like a sacrifice. It was very strange indeed. I just looked on in amazement.

Later on in the evening, I felt the power of God. It was the most exhilarating feeling I have ever felt before. I could see a shimmering golden light. I also had a vision of myself in the afterlife, where I was a spirit and was traveling through the universe with a feeling of total contentment and peace. I experienced a few more phenomenal events. Even though I had some great experiences, I wanted more evidence of God. I also figured that if there was a God, we must be able to have a better relationship between us. I did not have an answer to the truth of God yet. My time had not yet come.

I have had many other supernatural experiences. My own parents have experienced the supernatural world of spirits or demon-haunting, but like many, they just slough it off and don't think about it. I, being dedicated to the truth, must find out. What I found out in the end was awesome—and horrifying.

I was still not sure what the answer was, but I knew the supernatural world was real. I continued living in sin, waiting to see if one day God would reveal Himself to me in more certain terms. I needed facts and spiritual wisdom. To give my life to God, I needed to be 100 percent sure. At that point, I felt that there seemed to be a God, but the world was so messed up.

However, I did my due diligence to find the truth, and God rewarded me many years later. The rest of this book will show how I reached faith and knowledge of God. I am blessed now to be absolutely sure that there is a loving God. I share with you my journey to make the unknown known.

Chapter 2

God Shows Me the Truth, the Way, and the Life

The time had finally come for the Lord to show Himself to me. The greatest moments of my life were about to occur. By that time, I was about thirty-eight years old and was living a normal, comfortable life. I had a good job and a new girlfriend, Samantha, who would later become my wife and a witness to many miracles. I also had a beautiful daughter, whom I believe the Lord sent to me to show me unconditional love and to prepare me for the truth of love.

It all started one day when Samantha and I decided to find some books to read. We were going to go to the library, but we ended up at Goodwill, where we picked out several books. An attractive girl then mentioned that a book I'd chosen had had a great impact on her and that there was a companion book for it. The book was titled *The Celestine Prophecy* by James Redfield, it was eye-opening and full of wisdom. I talked to this female, and she mentioned that she wouldn't be working at the store much longer.

When I read the last sentence in the book, the Holy Spirit revealed to me that Jesus was the Son of God. I said to Samantha, "Jesus is the Son of God." It's remarkable to note that this book does not mention Jesus at all. God works in mysterious ways. I sometimes wonder—since God used this book to save me, and the girl had mentioned that she would be leaving soon—if the girl at the store might possibly have been an angel.

> *"Be not forgetful to entertain strangers: for thereby some have entertained angels unawares" (Hebrews 13:2).*

From that point on, Samantha and I had many miracles in our lives. Most coincidences are not coincidences but God working in our lives. I have coined a personal saying: "If it's a coincidence, then *that* is a coincidence."

At that time I gave my whole life to my Lord and Savior, Jesus. Still, there was much work to do and much wisdom to gain. The Holy Spirit then embraced me in power for about two weeks and gave me wisdom and testing. It was like a massive download of wisdom and information—more wisdom in two weeks than I'd gained in thirty-eight years of life on earth.

Chapter 3

I Meet the Devil

After the two weeks of testing and wisdom came the most fascinating encounter of my life. My former girlfriend came over with our young daughter, and she seemed distraught, complaining that her stomach was sore. I asked if I could try to heal her by faith. She got upset and became somewhat afraid. She seemed uncomfortable with my newfound faith. She told me she didn't believe that God operated in our day-to-day lives. I know otherwise. I now believe that she had a demonic influence of fear.

I stepped outside, and the commotion brought the neighbors over. Speaking in the Holy Spirit, I said that I loved them both, and they left. Then the police were called. I had only put my hands on my former girlfriend's forearms during the event, so there wasn't any real problem, but since I had mentioned God, I was taken to the hospital for a seventy-two-hour visit.

As I was waiting in the emergency room, it became apparent to me that this situation had been set up by the Lord, and I was being tested. Then I heard a voice, supernatural and evil. I now believe this entity was the Devil, in possesion of a willing host. At the time I just knew it was an evil presense that had to be dealt with. For a split second I marveled that God was showing me the supernatural in such power, but I didn't have time to ponder life at that time, for danger was at my door. In an instant, the Holy Spirit directed me to say, "In the name of Jesus, you are not permitted into my room." Then the evil entity was gone, for nothing can stand against the power of Jesus.

Being in the midst of a great spiritual test and in the lair of the Devil, it was important that I not fail. The Holy Spirit guided me all the way. I was shown not to eat their food or to sleep for as long as I was there. I was convinced that the doctor who came to see me was evil and served the dark side. He offered me pills, even though I was calm and polite and showed no signs of agitation. He went so far as to threaten me with an indefinite stay if I didn't take the pills. At that point, I dismissed the doctor and said I wouldn't talk to him anymore. I believe this was the doctor that allowed himself to be possessed by the evil entity who was most likely Satan.

They even tried to scare me with needles. They said, if you don't take the pills, we will strap you down in restraints and give you a needle. I said, "I will not consent to any drug." So they strapped me down on a gurney, and I closed my eyes and said, "Please, no," a couple of times. Then the medical personnel left the room. When they came back, they did not give me the needle.

I think this has some correlation to the fact that we all have the right to say no to evil. When the New World Order starts implanting people with chips, people's right to choose will be final. The Enemy will not be able to force a person to take the mark of the Beast. The threats they use will be powerless against faith in Jesus. They may be able to kill the body, but they have no rights to our souls.

My first night went well. If I started to sleep, I pinched myself, reminding myself that this was no joke, that the

Devil was lurking around my life. My weapons were faith in Jesus, fasting, **and** not sleeping. The second night, I think they were on to my success, because every time rolled over or made a significant movement, I heard a sound like a spoon stirring in a teacup. I was not sure what to make of that, except that "they" seemed to know I wasn't sleeping. It was a good thing I stayed awake, because during that second night, a disturbed man came into my room. I politely asked him to return to his own room, and he did so without incident.

During these hard times, the Lord gave me strength and visions. The light from the hallway made a V-shaped sign in my room. To me it was God saying that I was on my way to victory, that He was there with me and protecting me. The rest of the time progressed without incident. I was let out and returned home. I noticed that my lawn was covered in little purple flowers. I believe they were a gift or sign from God that I had passed the test.

However, my hardest tests were yet to come.

A Side Note

Interestingly, my daughter took a picture of her mother, and in the picture you can see what looks like a demon. You can't see my ex-girlfriend, but she was lying on the couch underneath this entity. (See the photo on the back cover.) She was dealing with demons, because she was involved with the occult and such things as tarot cards. These are tools of witchcraft. When you consult the spirit realm for the future or information, you tap into the demonic realm. The only way to get proper guidance regarding the future is to go to the only correct source: God.

> *"When someone tells you to consult mediums and spiritists, who whisper and mutter, should not a people inquire of their God? Why consult the dead on behalf of the living?"* (Isa. 8:19 NIV).

> *"Do not turn to mediums or seek out spiritists, for you will be defiled by them. I am the Lord your God"* (Lev. 19:31 NIV).

One of the reasons we separated was because she liked to drink alcohol. I hope and pray that she has that under control. I get concerned for people who get involved with such things as Ouija boards, psychics, astrology, fornication, and drunkenness—especially if they don't think it's a big deal, that it's all fun and games.

Here's what the Lord says about these exact things:

> *"Adultery, fornication, idolatry, witchcraft, drunkenness . . . They which do such things shall not inherit the kingdom of God"* (Gal. 5:19-21).

Today this world has made sin acceptable, fun, or even a right. Such things as astrology, Ouija boards, palm reading, and going to psychics are all considered witchcraft and should be avoided completely. If God wants you to know the future, He will show you. Do not take it upon yourself to play God.

I had two coincidences that were God's confirmation that I was on the right track in writing this book. On one particular day, I had written about occult practices. Afterward, I met with some people. The female was talking about channeling and occult powers. I warned her that she was dealing with the dark side, but she was adamant that she was right. I believe she had demonic influence. Right after I'd written about the subject, I was confronted on it.

A more pleasant coincidence—a small miracle, actually—also occurred that day. I had written the final words of my book on that same day, the day after Father's Day. My wife had given me a Father's Day card. When I opened it for the first time on the day after, I read a Bible verse on it, Matthew 5:16, which duplicated the sentiment of my final words. The two were almost identical, and the Scripture fit so well that I put it in between the words I had written. It was just another small coincidence that I believe the Lord used to show me I was on the right track with this book.

The problem with some people is that they want an instant answer. Sometimes patience is required by the Lord, but He will deliver the goods every time.

Chapter 4

The Devil's Plan

Since the Devil fell from grace, and Adam and Eve fell into sin, Satan has been given power to rule the world.

> *"and the whole world lies in the power of the evil one" (1 John 5:19 English Standard version)*

> *"the earth is given into the hand of the wicked" (Job 9:24 KJV)*

> *"The god of this world hath blinded the minds of them which believe not" (2 Cor. 4:4).*

> *"The prince of this world be cast out" (John 12:31).*

> *"For the prince of this world cometh" (John 14:30).*

> *"The prince of this world is judged" (John 16:11).*

That being the case, the world is full of deception and misery. We need to start dispelling the lies that we have been taught by this world. The powerful elite, from pharaohs to politicians of today, have all been a part of the lie being told to humanity. These elite rulers were Devil-worshippers back then, and unfortunately the elite are still worshipping the Devil today.

Back in ancient times, the Devil and demons were free to be worshipped in the open. The Mayans and Egyptians reported on these alien-like gods. Now, with technology, cameras, and a massive population, the Devil has changed his strategy from open worship of himself to convincing the modern populations that he isn't real. The old saying rings true here: "The greatest trick the Devil ever played was to fool people into believing he wasn't real."

Now we have to use history, the Holy Bible, and all other evidence to proceed. We know the Devil is ruler of this world and that he will he use his power to deceive mankind. One way to do so is to spread his evil gene.

> *"The sons of God (fallen angels) saw the daughters of men that they were fair; and they took them wives of all which they chose . . . (Gen 6:2 KJV)*
>
> *There were giants in the earth in those days; and also after that" (Gen 6:4 KJV)*

Giants are the offspring of demons or fallen angels. Today, instead of giants—but of the same evil gene pool— we have aliens. Aliens are nothing more than demons in disguise. One of the Devil's lies to humanity is that our ancestors are aliens and that they created us. These aliens are demonic hybrids. Some look like typical aliens, with big heads and big, black eyes. Some are reptilian in nature. Some of these evil hybrids can even shape-shift like their father the Devil. The Devil can transform himself into many identities.

> *"And no marvel; for Satan himself is trans-formed into an angel of light" (Rev. 11:14).*

This shows that the Devil has great abilities to deceive and manipulate. He has the ability to change form and likeness, hence the term *shape-shifter.*

Let's investigate what Satan's plan is. It is in the Bible, and the evidence is all around us in society. The goal is the same as that of any other tyrant: total power. Hitler started World War II and almost achieved world dominance. The Antichrist will bring about World War III and the New World Order. It is Satan's plan to enslave mankind with the mark of the Beast. Until modern times, such a mark would seem impossible. With technology, it is now possible to implant microchips in every human on earth. England has already made a law that says all pets must receive microchips. All of this is for the purpose of acclimating the masses to the idea of mandatory microchipping. I warn you now that there is a plan to "chip" every man, woman, and child. The Rockefellers, as well as many other elitists, have been open about their plans for microchipping people, with a goal to microchip everyone on earth.

Alex Jones is a web journalist who exposes the plans of the New World Order (NWO). He has interviewed Aaron

Russo, a famous Hollywood director, who has shared details of his conversations with elitist Nick Rockefeller. In this interview (available on the Internet), Russo talked about the elites' knowledge of 9/11 and the Iraq war that would follow. He talked of how the Rockefellers backed the women's liberation movement. The goal, however, was not to empower and create equality; it was to double the tax base, to break up the family, and to have children indoctrinated in schools.

The worst topic they discussed was the elitists' goal to microchip the "serfs." We are considered "useless eaters" and slaves to these evil elitists. Russo also said that after the "terrorist attack," they would have an "endless war on terror" so they could justify taking our rights away. Aaron Russo has since died.

I know that you risk your life if you stand up against the NWO. Many people have been murdered for speaking out. I think Aaron Russo has become martyr for truth. May God bless the people who stand up for truth and fight against tyranny. "The Patriot Act" was one of the resulting actions that took away freedom in exchange for the lie of safety. Renewed and signed by President Obama, it allows the government to spy and listen to our phone calls. Rockefeller has stated clearly that the goal of the elite is to have a New World Order, with total power and total corruption from the top of the pyramid.

I have heard many of our leaders and elite talk about this New World Order. Here are a few.

George Bush Sr., former president of the United States, said, "We have for us the opportunity to forge for ourselves and for future generations a New World Order . . . When we are successful—and *we will be*—we have a real chance at this New World Order, an order in which a credible United Nations can use its peacekeeping role to fulfill the promise and vision of the UN's founders." George Bush Sr. made this televised speech on 9/11, 1991. Numerology, astrology (calendar), and symbolism are just a few of the methods used by the ruling class. It is part of their witchcraft and occult involvement. The fact that George Bush Sr. made his "New World Order" speech 10 years to the date of the the World Trade Center attack is not a coincidence. The ruling class use planned terrorist attacks and wars to serve as a blood sacrifice to the Devil, and to hold on to power. These people are ultimately controlled by the Devil. They use symbols and numerology extensively in witchcraft, and their control over society. Bush said to Congress, "Out of these troubled times, our fifth objective—a New World Order—can emerge."

Here we see a former president of the United States talking about his globalist agenda. These leaders have no allegiance to their home countries. They are pushing for global United Nations control. We all know the saying: "Power corrupts, and absolute power corrupts absolutely."

Al Gore, former vice president of the United States said, "The climate bill will help to bring about *global governance*."

Barack Obama, current president of the United States, said, "All nations *must* come together to build a stronger *global regime*."

French president Chirac talked about the first component of an authentic global governance. "For the first time, humanity is instituting a genuine instrument of *global governance*."

S. Talbot, secretary of state under former US president Bill Clinton, said, "In the next century [which is now], nations as we know it will be obsolete; all states will recognize a *single global authority* and realize that national sovereignty wasn't such a great deal after all."

Mikhail Gorbachev, former Russian leader, said, "Further global progress is now possible only through a quest for universal consensus in the movement toward a *New World Order*."

Robert Mueller, former assistant attorney general of the United Nations, said, "We must move as quickly as possible to a *one-world government, one-world religion, under a one-world leader*."

Pope John Paul II said, "More than ever, we need a *new international order*."

David Rockefeller, elitist businessman, said at a 1991 Bilderberg meeting, "We are grateful to *The Washington Post, The New York Times, Time* magazine, and their great publications, whose directors have attended our meetings and respected their promises of discretion for almost forty years. It would have been impossible for us to develop our plan for the world if we had been subjected to the lights of publicity during those years. But the world is now more sophisticated and prepared to march toward *a world government*. The supranational sovereignty of an intellectual elite and world bankers is surely preferable to the national auto-determination practiced in past centuries." Taken out of his own autobiography, *Memoirs*, is this quote from page 405: "Some even believe we are part of a secret cabal working against the best interest of the United States, characterizing my family and me as "internationalists" and of conspiring with others around the world to build a more integrated global, political, and economic structure—one world, if you will. If that is the charge, I stand guilty, and I am proud of it."

Henry Kissinger, former secretary of state under President Richard Nixon, said, "Individual rights will be willingly relinquished for the guarantee of their well-being granted to them by the *World Government*."

Journalist Walter Cronkite said, "Any attempt to achieve world order before that time must be the work of the Devil. Well, join me. I'm glad to sit here at the right hand of Satan."

In 1976 Congressman Larry P. McDonald had this to say of the Rockefellers: "The drive of the Rockefellers and their allies is to create a one-world government, combining super-capitalism and communism under the same tent . . . Do I mean conspiracy? Yes, I do. I am convinced that there is such a plot, international in scope, generations old in the planning, and incredibly evil in intent."

John F. Hylan, mayor of New York from 1918 to 1925, said, "The real menace of our republic is this invisible government, which like a giant octopus sprawls its slimy length over city, state, and nation. Like the octopus of real life, it operates under cover of a self-created screen. At the head of this octopus are the Rockefeller Standard Oil interests and a small group of powerful banking houses generally referred to as international bankers. The little coterie of powerful international bankers virtually runs the US government for its own selfish purposes. They practically control both political parties."

Mayer Rothchild, elitist banker, said, "Give me control of a nation's money, and I care not who makes its laws."

Benjamin Disraeli, historic British prime minister, said, "Rothchild is the lord and master of the money markets of the world."

In 1950 James Warburg, a Rothchild banking agent, said, "We shall have world government whether or not you like it . . . by conquest or consent."

> Finally, Jesus will have the last word: *"For by the words thou shalt be justified, and by thy words thou shalt be condemned" (Matt. 13:37).*

These NWO globalists will create a scenario of famine, destruction, and war to bring about the solution of the NWO and global control by the banking elite. Don't fall for their scam. They are under the Devils control. They are liars and murderers, just like their master, Satan.

> *"No man might buy or sell, save he that had the mark, or the name of the beast, or the number of his name" (Rev. 13:17).*
>
> *And the number of the Beast is 666 (Rev. 13:18).*

For the NWO plan to work, they want a population that is under 500 million. This is where the Georgia Guidestones comes in.

A granite monument in Elbert County, Georgia, commissioned by R. C. Christian, the Georgia Guidestones describe the NWO plan for the world. These are rules by the elite. There are ten guides or laws written in eight popular languages, and they are somewhat shocking.

1. Maintain humanity under 500,000,000 in perpetual balance with nature. (That would mean culling the planet of about 5.5 billion people.)
2. Guide reproduction wisely, improving fitness and diversity. (This is eugenics; they will say who can reproduce.)
3. Unite humanity with a living new language. (This means one world order, one world government, one world religion, and one language.)
4. Rule passion, faith, tradition, and all things with tempered reason.
5. Protect people and nations with fair laws and just courts.
6. Let all nations rule internally resolving external disputes in a world court. (This is a push for world power.)
7. Avoid petty laws and useless officials.
8. Balance personal rights with social duties. (You will be a slave to the system.)
9. Prize truth, beauty, love, seeking harmony with the infinite.
10. Be not a cancer on the earth; leave room for nature. (In other words, we must stop the spread of human parasites on earth.)

This is the agenda of the New World Order. They throw in some nice comments about love and justice to throw us off. Their plan is to wipe out a large portion of society so they can easily control the remaining population. They cannot achieve their goals with so many people. Their goal is to make you a slave when you take the 666 mark of the Beast. You will lose your soul, should you take that mark.

Their major power lies with government. They control the military. They control the banks and money. That's why we are constantly at war. It is standard procedure for evil tyrants. They create a problem and then offer their solution. Many wars were started with false flag attacks. This means that the elite cause the problem and then blame another so they can fulfill their goals. Hitler used this tactic when he burned down the Reichstag and blamed his opposition. He then gained more power and started World War II.

The Vietnam War was started over an incident in the Gulf of Tonkin that didn't take place.

Recently, 9/11 was used to begin the war in Iraq. This act, I believe, was an inside job. Someone lied about weapons of mass destruction. I won't go into detail about the 9/11 false flag attack, but you should review the evidence. It clearly shows 9/11 to be an inside job by some secret organization within the US government. Once you realize that 9/11 was perpetrated by our own, it will open your eyes to the level of evil and corruption at the very top levels.

Hitler said, "If you tell a lie big enough, and keep repeating it, people will eventually come to believe it." I warn you now that nothing has changed from Hitler's time. We are still controlled by these power-hungry megalomaniacs. They are, in turn, controlled by their master, Satan.

The US government is run by these Luciferian Freemasons. The laws they are passing are unconstitutional. They are doing things in secret that are unbelievable but true. There are reports and videos of hundreds of empty concentration camps, waiting to be filled by ordinary citizens. There has been a record amount of ammunition acquired by the Department of Homeland Security. We are talking about millions of rounds of hollow-point bullets. What does Homeland Security know that the public doesn't? These bullets are made to kill, to do the most damage to the target. They wouldn't be used for target practice or anything other than murder. There are hundreds of thousands of "bio-caskets," stored in fields around the United States. These caskets can hold around three or four bodies each.

The armed forces are now doing martial law drills in all the major US cities. It used to be against the law for the army to police the public. In 1878 the Posse Comitatus Act was made law. It stated that the army could not police the public as was done in banana republics. Now the army can be seen everywhere in domestic issues. This is the beginning of the military police state. They try to sell safety and security in exchange for your freedom. Meanwhile, they are the ones infringing on your safety and security in the first place.

Benjamin Franklin said, "Those who would sacrifice freedom for security deserve neither."

The list of evil crimes these leaders have committed is almost endless. Putting fluoride in drinking water is nothing short of poisoning people. Fluoride may be good for your teeth, but it is poisonous when ingested. There is much evidence of "chem-trails," the government's spraying of cities with unknown chemicals—most likely a poison to make us docile and infertile. When someone tries to deceive us, it helps to put a little truth in the story so that it sells.

Beware of government vaccinations in this day and age. We have seen the benefits in eradicating some diseases, but when they use vaccinations for their purposes, they may *give* you the disease instead. In 1918 the vaccinations for the Spanish flu killed more people than it saved. Giving you a small dose of the disease is no guarantee that you will not get severe symptoms and die rather than build an immunity as the vaccine was supposedly intended.

Barack Obama has signed 157 executive orders, as of the writing of this book. These are undemocratic decrees made without debate that are normally passed in times of war or disaster. Here are some orders that will give you a clue as to what the government plan is for society. These are some of the most egregious orders.

- Executive Order (EO) 11004: Housing and Finance to relocate communities and build new housing with public funds and to designate areas to be abandoned.
- EO 1005: Railroads, waterways, and public storage facilities to be under full control of the government. (I would like to point out that these storage facilities would make a perfect temporary jail. They are normally fenced with barbed wire, and all the units have locks.)

- EO 11921: Gives the Federal Emergency Preparedness Agency power to take control of financial institutions. It also states that when the president calls for a state of emergency, congress cannot review the action for six months.
- EO 13575: Rural Council to take control of farms.
- EO 10990: Allows the government to take over all modes of transportation and control highways and seaports.
- EO 10997: Allows the government to take control of all electrical power, gas, petroleum, fuel, and minerals.
- EO 10995: Allows the government to seize and control the communication media.
- EO 11000: Allows the government to mobilize civilians into work brigades under government supervision.

These are some of the most offensive executive orders. It is obvious that the government knows of and is planning for major changes. These tyrants are taking away our freedoms every day. Soon it will be much worse. Please prepare yourselves and reach out to your family and neighbors. Most importantly, reach out to God.

Chapter 5

The Devil's Accomplices

The Devil has an intricate web of power over this world. Many people from the world of politicians, bankers, businessmen, musicians, and the media worship evil and promote the New World Order. The Devil's wicked bloodline has infected the world. The powerful elite at the head of the Illuminati are dedicated to devil worship, and some have tainted, evil blood. The human race is always at war, because our leaders are always corrupted by blood or by power.

Here are a few unbelievable facts. All US presidents have "royal" blood, meaning that they are reptilian "blue bloods." Obama, Cheney, Bush, and Vlad the Impaler (Dracula) are all related by blood. Not only is John Kerry a blood relative to George Bush, but they both were in the secret society Skull and Bones. The fact that they shared a ballot when running for president is no coincidence. It shows that we are given a semblance of freedom, when in fact we are being controlled and manipulated.

We do not have a choice in electing our leaders; they are chosen and groomed for years in advance. The world's elite bankers choose the two leading candidates so that one of their own men always wins. John F. Kennedy was the last US president who stood for real freedom, and he was assassinated for it. He was in the process of giving back to the people—the rightful owners—the power to issue currency. We have been set up and lied to. We do not have the freedom we think we have. The elite have manipulated society from the start. Many of the founding fathers of the United States were Freemasons, and many are Freemasons today. I am sorry to inform my brothers and sisters that we have been told many lies to deceive us.

Many of our leaders have literally sold their souls for power and money. Many of these leaders are hybrids by blood, and the others are humans who have given themselves over to demons. These fallen angels and their offspring are responsible for unexplained phenomena such as UFOs and UFO abductions, pyramids, magic, and many ghost stories. These demonic giants were the only ones capable of building the great pyramids and other wonders of the world. It is noteworthy that many civilizations have pyramids; they are not limited to Egypt and Mexico. This also explains the perpetuation of horrible blood sacrifice of children to evil gods.

Such civilizations are far distant in time, yet they have many characteristics in common with modern civilization, including their gods. In past times, these beings showed themselves out in the open, and that is why we have descriptions of the Devil and his demons. During my research, I learned of a man who made a video testimony. He actually met Anubis, the Egyptian god with the head of a dog—for real, not in a dream or vision. Anubis wanted this man's soul, but the Lord told the man, "Say you belong to Me." The man told Anubis, "You can have my body, but my soul belongs to Jesus. After that, Anubis had to leave under the power of God.

The first of these civilizations was the Sumerians. They wrote about their ancient gods called the *anunnaki*. *Anunnaki* means "those who from the heavens came." *Anu* is the Devil, and the anunnaki are the fallen angels. In the Sumerian texts, it is reported that these beings literally came down from the sky in a flying vehicle. These were the first UFO/alien sightings. The difference is that, back in ancient times, these evil beings were visible and in direct communication with the people. Nowadays they have gone into hiding, but they are still worshipped by and in communication with our elitist, Luciferian leaders. It is interesting that the god Anubis has the word *anu* in his name. You see here a connection that gathers all the mythologies into one picture of truth.

Let's look at the similarities of these ancient cultures. Their stories couldn't line up as they do unless they were true. The fact is that the Devil and fallen angels have been here all along. Ancient mythology confirms the Bible's truth. There are engraved pictures of a bird-headed god in Sumerian tablets. This corresponds to the Mayan god *Quetzalcoatl*, which means "feathered serpent." Satan is a serpent. He is also a bird-headed god. Another coincidence? I think not.

> *"And the great dragon was cast out, that old serpent, called the Devil" (Rev. 12:9).*

Chinese mythology is filled with dragons, and they have pyramids as well. How can civilizations from across the world have the same gods, the same pyramids, and the same basic mythology? They all relate the truth of the Bible, which speaks of the Nephilim and Rapheim.

> *"There we saw the giants . . . and we were in our own sight as grasshoppers" (Num. 13:33).*

> *"There were giants on the earth in those days; and also after that" (Gen. 6:4).*

The Illuminati-controlled media do not want you to know the truth. They will not report on the finding of giant human skeletons that have been found across the earth.

Another lie is being told of the extinction of dinosaurs millions of years ago. The facts is, dinosaurs were recorded by the Romans on petroglyphs. In South America, pottery resembling dinosaurs has been discovered. God talked to Job about the *behemoth* and described the brontosaurus. He also spoke of the *leviathan*.

> *"Behemoth . . . he eateth grass like an ox . . . He moveth his tail like a cedar . . . his bones are as strong pieces of brass, his bones are like bars of iron . . . he drinketh up a river" (Job 40:15-24).*

> *"Canst thou draw out leviathan with a hook?" (Job 41:1).*

Remember: the elite wants you to be ignorant slaves. This is a giant lie.

The deception of the masses continues unabated with one of their worst lies: the alien connection. These evil entities have not gone away. They now show themselves as aliens from another world. They know that the populations of the modern world will not fall down and worship outright evil, so they have developed another strategy. They will deceive many into believing that the demonic "aliens" are here to help us. They may also use UFO phenomena as a threat, implying that we have no choice but to follow such a powerful adversary. This is one method they will use to bring about the New World Order.

If you think of the sheer numbers of UFO sighting and abductions, no reasonable person can dismiss every account. The question is: what are they, and what is their intention? During these end times, it's no wonder there are so many sightings and abductions. The Devil is rallying his troops for the final battle detailed in Revelation, the last book of the Holy Bible. We are all nearing the greatest battle of all time. This is another David-and-Goliath story, where the odds are against us, but with Jesus, we are victorious.

Any group that meets in secret and binds their members to secrecy is likely involved in Luciferian doctrine. I will briefly describe the largest known secret organizations. They are: the Illuminati, the Freemasons, the Bilderberg Group, the Council on Foreign Relations, and David Rockefeller's Trilateral Commission. All these groups have one thing in common: they are evil, and they want a one-world government.

In his book, *FDR: My Exploited Father-in-Law*, Curtis Bean Dall wrote: "Most of his thoughts were carefully manufactured for him in advance by the Council on Foreign Relations, a one-world money group. The United Nations is but a long-range, international banking apparatus, clearly set up for financial and economic profit by a small group of powerful, one-world revolutionaries, hungry for profit and power. The one-world government leaders and their ever close bankers have now acquired full control of the money and credit machinery of the U.S., via the creation of the privately owned Federal Reserve."

Barry Goldwater, US senator in 1964, said, "The Trilateral Commission is intended to be the vehicle for mufti-national consolidation of the commercial and banking interests by seizing control of the political government of the U.S. . . . They will rule the future."

The Illuminati consists of many powerful groups. The Bilderberg Group is one of those top-secret organizations. They meet in secrecy and under heavy security. In their membership are the most powerful people in the world. Royalty, government officials, and world bankers all plot against humanity for their own greed and power. They delegate to other groups—like the Council on Foreign Relations, the Freemasons, and so on—to bring about their plan for a New World Order.

Many are deep into satanic doctrine. That is why in the United States you still see demonic symbolism everywhere, such as pyramids, obelisks, and snakes on the medical symbol. The elite world bankers control US politicians and still worship the evil symbols of the Devil. Hence the pyramid is on the dollar, and the obelisk is displayed in Washington, DC.

There is also a hidden owl on the dollar bill. The owl represents Molech, who is the Devil. In ancient times, people sacrificed children to this deity. Many politicians and leaders from around the world participate in Cremation of Care at the Bohemian Grove. These respected, mostly older men dress up in black robes in front of a giant owl and do a mock sacrifice. This sounds incredible and unbelievable, but it has been caught on video for anyone who wants to know the truth about our leaders.

All these secret organizations are interconnected, and their end goal is world domination. Their plan is to microchip everyone, just as the Bible states. They will try to cull humanity to a manageable number, and the remaining individuals will be offered the "mark of the Beast." If a person does not take the microchip mark of the Beast, he will be murdered. If he does take the microchip, he will lose his soul forever.

> *"And that no man might buy or sell, save he that had the mark, or the name of the beast, or the number of his name (666)" (Rev. 13:17).*

Albert Pike was a famous thirty-three-degree Grand Master Freemason. He also created the Southern Masonic Scottish Rite Order. When one is near the top level of thirty-three-degree Freemasonry, he is definitely informed that Lucifer is the Freemason god. Many at lower degrees of Freemasonry may not be aware of the Freemason goals and the real truth behind their secret organization.

In 1871 Albert Pike wrote a letter to Giuseppe Mazzini regarding three world wars that would take place to try to bring about a New World Order. This letter was displayed in the British Museum Library until 1977. Mazzini was an Italian revolutionary leader in the 1800s, and he was also the director of the Illuminati. This letter foretells three world wars that must take place before the Illuminati (Freemasons) can take full control of the world via New World Order.

World War I was intended to destroy the power of the czars of Russia and to make Russia into a communist, atheistic state. The Illuminati have no state allegiance. Their only goal is to serve Lucifer and to bring in the NWO, which is world domination. They used this war to destroy nations and to weaken religion. Their goal was accomplished.

World War II was meant to bring about a Jewish nation in Palestine. The Illuminati wanted communism to balance Christianity. Communism, created by the Illuminati, is intended to suppress Christianity until the time when the Illuminati will try to use it to their advantage, blaming Christianity for all the troubles in the world that the Illuminati have created. This will occur during the last upheaval and social cataclysm that will be forced on society in the last days.

The third world war in Pike's letter will be the last war foretold. This is the final battle to implement their NWO scheme. This part of the letter foretells the war between Islam and the Jewish nation. We can clearly see that in the present day.

Here is an excerpt from that letter: "Then everywhere, the citizens, obliged to defend themselves against the world minority of revolutionaries, will exterminate those destroyers of civilization, and the multitude, disillusioned with Christianity, whose deistic spirits will from that moment be without compass or direction, anxious for an ideal, but without knowing where to render its adoration, will receive the true light through the universal manifestation of the pure doctrine of Lucifer brought finally out in the public view." The letter goes on to describe how they want to destroy Christianity and atheism.

These secret societies worship Lucifer. I have listened to a Shriner describe how Lucifer is the angel of light and wisdom. These groups have a Luciferian agenda of world domination. They will succeed in their plans, because the Holy Bible confirms that these times must occur before Jesus can return to destroy evil. Now is the time to call out to Jesus—before these terrible times begin.

Albert Pike's anagram is "TRAP BEE ILK." I believe that bees are symbolic of humanity. There has been a large crop circle of a bee. We need bees to pollinate most of our crops. In the last few years, there has been a disturbing disappearance of bee colonies. The "zombie parasite" that kills bees has been discovered. Nicki Minaj, an Illuminati-puppet singer, has a CD entitled *Beez in the Trap*.

All the facts and evidence clearly show a conspiracy of elitist manipulation that controls *you* and the world. Time is short. Get prepared. Research and pray.

Chapter 6

The Devil's Symbols

You may have noticed the increase in hand gestures among our entertainers, leaders, and politicians. Satanism has become mainstream in our society. Everyone knows that the inverted cross is a satanic symbol. The Illuminati take an evil symbol and say it means something else. Then society unknowingly replicates the symbol. Let's look at the more subtle ones.

The "peace sign" is also known as the "broken cross" or witch's foot. It is actually an upside-down cross with the arms broken down. The "okay" sign is used by the followers of Satan, with the hand actually making a 666. The pyramid sign is also gaining momentum. You will see many entertainers flashing the pyramid sign with their hands. They are showing their allegiance to Satan, while at the same time corrupting our children and society.

Another sign is called the "horned owl" or "Devil's horns." That is when someone holds their hand up with the index finger and little finger pointing up. This represents the Devil's horns—or the owl, which represents Molech. This sign shows allegiance to him and is also intended to put curses on targeted victims. *Molech* is an another name for Satan. People have sacrificed their children in fire to Molech.

You may have noticed that many entertainers cover one eye in their pictures. This action shows their allegiance to

Satan's all-seeing eye, which is shown on the US dollar. When they put the index finger to their mouths, they are saying, "Shh, don't tell anyone our evil secrets."

"And thou shalt not let any of thy seed pass through the fire to Molech" (Lev. 18:21).

This is the same god that the elite worship today. From presidents to wealthy businessman, they go to the Bohemian Grove where they do mock sacrifice and worship the Devil. You can only imagine what horrible rituals they do in private.

Start to notice all of the evil imagery put before us by our governments, corporations, and the entertainment industry. When you see these signs and logos, know that the one sending it to you is an evil Illuminati puppet. These people are out there to deceive you and to enslave mankind. The evidence of this conspiracy is clearly shown on the US dollar bill. The use of the number thirteen is extensively used. There are thirteen blocks on the pyramid, thirteen leaves on the olive branch, thirteen stripes, thirteen arrows, thirteen berries, and thirteen stars. Two of the Latin phrases have thirteen letters. Thirteen, as we know, is unlucky . . . but why?

Thirteen is described by many mythologies as unlucky. The Bible states,

"But in the thirteenth year they rebelled," (Gen. 14:4).

There are reported to be thirteen families who head the Illuminati. They are rebels against the Lord, the same as Satan. It makes no sense that Americans would put a pyramid on US money, but when you understand the symbolism behind it, it makes sense. The ones who put the pyramid on the US dollar worship the same gods as the ancient Egyptians and Mayans. These Illuminati designed the "all-seeing eye" on the pyramid's capstone. This represents the eye of Lucifer or the eye of Horus, an ancient Egyptian god. That is also why you will notice that single-eye imagery is prevalent in media and logos, and all the top entertainers are flashing the symbols. This is what our children are being indoctrinated in. Evil cult signs and symbols abound in society.

On the bill it says in Latin, "Novus Ordo Seclorum." Above that it says, "Annuit Coeptis," which together states loosely: "The new world order is a crowned success." The feathers on the eagle represent the levels of Freemasonry. There are thirty-three feathers on one side of the eagle and thirty-two on the other, each representing degrees of freemasonry. There are nine feathers on the tail that stand for the ninth-degree of Scottish Rite Freemasonry.

There are also hidden pictures on the US dollar bill. There is an owl, which we already discussed as a symbol of Molech, the Devil. The year on the bill is 1776, which some people think represents the year of American independence. The real reason for its placement is that the Illuminati was created that year. George Washington was a thirty-third-degree Freemason. The streets in Washington, DC, are designed with the occult in mind. You can see for yourself that the White House sits at the bottom of a satanic pentagram. There is also an owl design. The U.S. Pentagon is the shape made inside of a pentagram. The pentagram is extensively used by satanic organizations.

There is overwhelming evidence to prove the evil nature of this world and its leaders. Don't fall into the trap they have set for us all. Many of us are stuck in a "normalcy bias," which is where we have lived a certain way for so long that we can't conceive of our lives confronting disaster. Most of this world is living in fear and denial, not wanting to face the tremendous evidence of such negative prospects. Stand up and face the truth now, while there is time to prepare.

Many in the spotlight have seen only the partial truth. They have been blinded by their own lust for power and fame. They know the truth of Satan, but they are deceived into believing that Satan is still an angel of light and that there are no consequences for serving him. These groups have sold their souls for power, fortune, and fame. Amazingly, many famous people are coming out now and saying they have sold their souls for fame. Here are a few.

On *60 Minutes*, Bob Dylan explained to Ed Bradley how he sold his soul.

Kanye West said he sold his soul at one of his concerts. "I sold my soul to the Devil. I know it was a crappy deal."

In an interview, Katy Perry said, "So I sold my soul to the Devil."

On a late-night talk show, Roseanne Barr described selling her soul.

In a video on the Internet, Snooki explained why she sold her soul.

These people know the Devil and are speaking out. They are dead serious. Corporate logos and hand gestures are sophisticated gang signs to these elitists. They are hidden in plain sight.

God likes to be more subtle. I've noticed that God uses creation to give us insight into who He is. God is triune, consisting of (1) the Father, (2) the Son, and (3) the Holy Spirit. It is apparent that God uses His own perfect nature to build a universe with these triad characteristics. After God, man consists of (1) body, (2) mind, and (3) spirit. Then we can go down to the molecular level. The atom is the building block for all matter, including people. There are three components to an atom: (1) protons, (2) neutrons, and (3) electrons. Another group of three consists of (1) animals, (2) plants, and (3) minerals. Everything about God, man, and the microscopic atom has three parts, yet they are one.

Here is an interesting quote from Arthur Young, born in 1741: "God sleeps in the minerals, awakens in plants, walks in animals, and thinks in man."

Chapter 7

Economics of Destruction

There is an elephant in the room. It's called the US debt.

In 1989 there was a debt of three trillion dollars.

In 1999 the US debt was five trillion dollars.

In 2008 the US debt was over nine trillion dollars.

As of 2013, the US debt is seventeen trillion dollars.

You can see the pattern. There is no effort to fix this problem. The world bankers want to destroy sovereign money so they can bring about the New World Order currency.

One out of every six people in the United States is now living in poverty. Approximately one out of every six workers in the United States is a federal or state employee. This shows the gigantic size of the US government. To understand the magnitude of the problem, we have to determine how we got to this point.

Creation of the Federal Reserve Bank was the beginning of the end for the US dollar. It was created in 1913, and it now gives a private banking consortium the power to print money. So the power of the people has now been usurped by a group of international bankers who are Illuminati.

Senator Barry Goldwater stated, "The accounts of the Federal Reserve system have never been audited. It operates outside the control of Congress and manipulates the credit of the United States."

In 1913 Congressman Charles Lindbergh Sr. said this about the Federal Reserve Act: "The worst legislative crime of the ages is perpetrated by this banking and currency bill. From now on, depressions will be scientifically created." In 1923 he said, "The financial system has been turned over to the Federal Reserve Board. That Board administers the finance system by authority of a purely profiteering group. The system is *private*, conducted for the sole purpose of obtaining the greatest possible profits from the use of other people's money."

In 1932 Congressman Louis T. McFadden said, "We have, in this country, one of the most corrupt institutions the world has ever known. I refer to the Federal Reserve Board. This evil institution has impoverished the people of the United States and practically bankrupted our government. It has done this through the corrupt practices of the moneyed vultures who control it. There is not a man within the sound of my voice who does not know that this nation is run by the international bankers. Some people think the Federal Reserve Bank is a government institution. It is not a government institution. They are private credit monopolies which prey upon the people of the United States for the benefit of themselves and their foreign swindlers."

James A. Garfield, former US president, said, "Whoever controls the volume of money in any country is absolute master of all industry and commerce."

Woodrow Wilson, former US president, said, "Our system of credit is concentrated in the hands of a few men. We have come to be one of the worst ruled, one of the most completely controlled and dominated governments of the world. No longer a government of free opinion, no longer a government of conviction and vote of the majority, but a government by the opinion and duress of small groups of dominant men."

Thomas Jefferson, founding father and third president of the United States, said,

"I sincerely believe the banking institutions, having the issuing power of money, are more dangerous to liberty than standing armies."

Abraham Lincoln said, "I have two great enemies, the southern army in front of me, and the bankers in the rear. Of the two, the one on my rear is my greatest foe."

James Madison, the fourth US president, said, "History records that *money changers* have used every form of abuse, intrigue, deceit, and violent means possible to maintain their control over governments by controlling money and its issuance."

The only time I remember in the Holy Bible where Jesus became violent and angry was when he overturned the money changers' tables at the temple (Matt 21:12). These money changers (bankers) were evil back then, and they are still the same today.

Henry Ford said, "It is well that the people of the nation do not understand our banking and monetary system, for if they did, I believe there would be a revolution before tomorrow morning."

Another nail in the coffin of the US dollar was the removal of the gold standard. The US dollar has now become a fiat currency. Fiat currency has no intrinsic value. You can no longer trade your dollars for real gold. The dollar has just become an IOU piece of paper. I would like to point out that every civilization that has used fiat currency has been overthrown and destroyed. Overnight, the dollar and financial markets can collapse. It is a question of *when* it will happen, not *if* it will happen.

> *"The merchants of the earth shall weep and mourn over her; for no man buyeth their merchandise any more" (Rev. 18:11).*

> *"Two pounds of wheat for a day's wages" (Rev 6:6 NIV).*

> *"For nation will rise against nation, and kingdom against kingdom: and there shall be famines, and pestilences, and earthquakes, in diverse places" (Matt 24:7).*

One of the greatest scams the US government inflicted on the world was the petro-dollar. They made a deal with OPEC and the oil producing nations that, to buy oil on the world market, they had to pay in US dollars. So the US dollar was artificially propped up. Today, many nations, including Russia, China, and Iran, are making new agreements so they don't have to buy US dollars. This is one of the real reasons the US invaded Iraq. Saddam Hussein wanted to trade in euros instead of US dollars. The war was started to keep control of the petro-dollar. The US government needed a better excuse than that to start a war, so they initiated the attack on 9/11. Otherwise, the nations of the world would not have stood by and watched; they would have acted in opposition.

The European Union is also in a dire financial situation. Only Germany is doing well, while the rest are near bankruptcy. How can small economies in the EU compete with Germany? They can't. The Union is doomed to fail. It's hard to say who will fall first, but when it happens, it will surely drag down the other nations of the world.

Dragon monument in Slovenia. Not only do the Asians worship the dragon. There are <u>13</u> boundary dragons in London England. The Welsh flag has a red dragon. Fascinating how all around the world, the leaders and elitists have built great and expensive monuments that idolize the dragon, who is clearly the devil. *NIV Rev 20:2 "He seized the dragon, that ancient serpent, who is the devil, or Satan"*

Two pictures of obelisks. You can see that the rulers of the U.S are still worshipping the same monuments to the devil that the ancient Egyptians did. Obelisks have been built by Freemasons in the U.S. Britain and France, which is the stronghold of the N.W.O.

A pyramid with an all seeing eye was put on the U.S dollar by the secret society called Freemasons. Almost all of the U.S presidents were Freemasons, with royal bloodlines. That's not a real democracy. These secret organizations control almost everything. The pyramid is a symbol of worship and allegiance to the devil. Ancient Egyptian (devil) worship is alive and well today thanks to the Freemasons and Illuminati. You will also notice many in the entertainment industry that are flashing the pyramid sign with their hands. This shows their allegiance to the N.W.O English translation of the Latin phrase Novus Ordo Seclorum is "A New Order of the Ages" or another words New World Order.

(top of page) Ram gargoyle (devil) on the National Cathedral, Washington DC. (bottom of page) Egyptian ram sphinx. The baphomet is a goat representation of the devil. The devil is also a shape-shifter, from dragon, serpent, goat or ram, bird etc. he can even transform himself into an angel of light.

(top of page) Snake gargoyle on the National Cathedral, Washington DC. (bottom page) Mayan snake. Both these pictures show worship and homage to a lowly snake. Mayans got their wisdom from the devil. That is why they have accomplished amazing feats of engineering and astronomy. They also sacrificed many to the devil.

This picture depicts an Egyptian giant behind a human figure. There are numerous mentions of giants in the Bible. These demonic giants of old, are now representing themselves to the world as "aliens" Another ploy to deceive mankind.

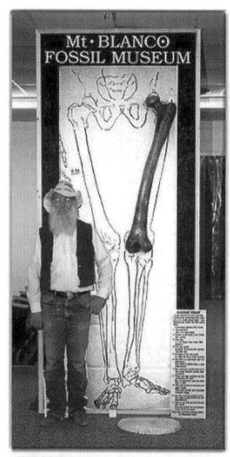

47 inch Human Femur

In the late 1950s, during road construction in south-east Turkey in the Euphrates Valley, many tombs containing the remains of Giants were uncovered. At two sites the leg bones were measured to be about 120 cms "47.24 inches". Joe Taylor, Director of the Mt. BLANCO FOSSIL MUSEUM in Crosbyton, Texas, was commissioned to sculpt this anatomically correct, and to scale, human femur. This "Giant" stood some 14-16 feet tall, and had 20-22 inch long feet. His or Her finger tips, with arms to their sides, would be about 6 feet above the ground. The Biblical record, in Deuteronomy 3:11 states that the Iron Bed of Og, King of Bashan was 9 cubits by 4 cubits or approximately 14 feet long by 6 feet wide!

GENESIS 6:4

There were Nephilim (Giants) in the earth in those days; and also after that when the sons of God (Angels?) came in unto the daughters of men, and they bare children to them, the same became mighty men which were of old, men of renown.

More Info & Replicas available at mtblanco1@aol.com or www.mtblanco.com
Mt. Blanco Fossil Museum • P.O. Box 559, Crosbyton, TX 79322 • 1-800-367-7454

This is a replica of a giants femur bone. Many giant bones have been discovered but the mainstream media owned by the satanic elitists will never report on such matters. Their job is to misinform you, and keep you ignorant of the truth.

Ancient Egyptian gods (demons) Thoth, Anubis etc. Plenty of demonic imagery. The eye of Horus, or all seeing eye of the devil. The owl is another representation of the devil or Molech. Bird headed gods are depicted by both Egyptian, Mayan, Aztec and more.

The devil has infiltrated many churches including the
Roman Catholic Church.

Buddha 666 hand gesture, way before it was used for an OK sign. The OK handsign makes three sixes. These deceivers of men will take an evil sign and then give it another meaning, therefore disguising the real intent.

Statue of man doing the satanic hand gesture "devils horns" and a dragon (devil) on his chest-plate. This is also before the "devils horns" were used for sign language and "rock n roll" Again these people take a satanic hand gesture and change the meaning so it becomes mainstream and unrecognizable to the general population. You will see politicians and entertainers flashing the devils horns. It is used to show allegiance to the devil or to put curses on intended victims.

These are Freemason symbols. (top of page) The dividers make a pyramid shape and an eye on top. The square is also in the shape of an inverted pyramid. (bottom of page) this symbol shows the all seeing eye within a pyramid. Also the rays of the sun emanate from the logo. This is because these people still worship the pagan sun god.

(top of page) Pentagrams are used extensively in satanic worship and ritual. Another deceit where the elite promote a symbol and make it mainstream (the star) but is used in secret ceremonies as the pentagram. (bottom of page) The U.S. Pentagon is the shape inside of a pentagram.

Asian temple dragon. Another clear picture of the devil as a dragon

This gargoyle that sits on the Notre Dame Cathedral in Paris looks similar to the actual photograph of a demon, on the back cover of this book. As the old adage goes "hidden in plain sight" There is an enormous amount of homage to demonic figures right out in the open. Idolatry to evil figures is commonplace around the world.

Chapter 8

Planet X, Nibiru, and Wormwood

Something astronomical approaches. NASA acknowledges the possibility of Planet X. In ancient mythology, it is called Nibiru. The Holy Bible calls it Wormwood. What does all this mean? Prevalent evidence shows that the elite know that something large and devastating exists. We have DUMBs (deep underground military bases) and seed banks all over the world.

> *"Hid themselves in the dens and in the rocks of the mountains" (Rev. 6:15).*

There is even a television show called *Doomsday Preppers* about people who are preparing for some apocalypse scenario. Many of these people are Christians; perhaps they know something the average person doesn't. My favorite list of popular "truth-ers" are Alex Jones, David Icke, Jesse Ventura, and Nigel Farage. Many more deserve mention, but these men have top venues to express and expose the truth. They do a great job, and I would recommend that people listen to them.

Nibiru is the name of our tenth planet, written about by the first advanced culture, the Sumerians. Thousands of years ago, they knew that the planets were round. Their pictures and writings show an extra planet in our solar system. This planet has a 3,600-year elliptical orbit. This planet is supposed to have a debris field of countless asteroids. The math shows that perhaps this is what caused the great flood of Noah's time. Planet X was discovered by NASA in the 1980s, but it was scrubbed from the news soon afterward. The Bible speaks of "Wormwood" and of objects falling from the sky.

> *"And there fell upon men a great hail out of heaven, every stone about the weight of a talent [70 pounds]" (Rev. 16:21).*

Ancient mythology, science, history, and the Holy Bible all corroborate and prove one truth. They all give evidence of each other. I urge readers to verify this information so they can be prepared for the disastrous events soon to take place. We all need to be spiritually ready for our Lord's return, so we can can live in abundance and without fear.

Chapter 9

My Vision of Hell

When I had my vision of hell, I didn't realize what it was at the time. I was off to the dentist to have my wisdom teeth out. I assumed that the dentist had given me an overdose of nitrous oxide gas, but either way I had a vision. I lost all control of my functions, and all I could see was a black-and-white haze, the kind you see on a TV with no reception, all black-and-white distortion. It was an awful feeling of having no control, of being alone.

In my later years of researching hell, I heard a man's story that sounded similar to my own but had more detail. He died in a casino and awoke to an all-white room, just nothingness everywhere—no body, no sound, just emptiness. He started to panic, and God said to him, "This is your eternity." Even though he believed in God, he still had gone to hell. He had gone to hell because, although he believed in Jesus, he didn't pay any attention to the Lord or worship Him. Then the Lord gave him a second chance. The man asked, "How do I keep from ever coming to this place again?" God replied, "*Get to know Me.*"

My own experience was dreadful, lasting only seconds, but I can imagine what an eternity in hell would be like. I don't know if our stories of eternal hell are true or not, but I do know for sure that hell has fire and torment. There seems to be a tiered system in hell. The worse you are on earth, the worse torment you receive in hell. More likely, hell will be torment by fire and other horrible punishment. The important part of this story is to *get to know God*. Don't just say you believe and live your own way. Seek Jesus. He is your only protection against hell, the Devil, and evil.

> *"The lake of fire is the second death"*
> *(Rev. 20:14).*

> *"There will be weeping and gnashing of teeth"*
> *(Luke 13:28).*

> *"And fear not them which kill the body, but are*
> *not able to kill the soul; but rather fear Him*
> *which is able to destroy both soul and body in*
> *hell" (Matt. 10:28).*

> *"So then because thou art lukewarm, and*
> *neither cold nor hot, I will spew thee out of*
> *my mouth" (Rev. 3:16).*

In other words, don't be a lukewarm Christian that God would rather spit out. Be passionate about God. Pray to Him. You can have a personal relationship with the Creator of the universe. God wants and expects this from us. He is waiting to give us love, forgiveness, and a new start.

I also want to point out that God is love. He is also justice and truth. If we are to know God, we have to look at justice and punishment. We must pay attention to His perfect justice and punishment.

> *"Behold the goodness and severity of God"*
> *(Rom. 11:22).*

Very important to learning and wisdom is fear of the Lord. Many people say they don't want to fear their God. We are all sinners, and we would all be judged guilty, if not for Jesus' sacrifice on the cross. What's important here is what God thinks and says, not how we feel. Think about how many different beliefs and ideas there are about the real truth of the world. There can only be one real truth, and that is God's truth.

> *"Fear of the Lord is the beginning of wisdom"*
> *(Ps. 111:10).*

Once you grasp this truth, more wisdom will be bestowed on you.

In John 14:6, Jesus said,

> *"I am the way, the truth and the life; no man cometh unto the Father, but by me."*

Jesus is the only truth. He is the only way to receive forgiveness and to spend eternity in heaven. Our spirits live forever, either in heaven or in hell. God's promise of eternal life is written in

> *Titus 1:2, which says, "In hope of eternal life, which God, that cannot lie, promised before the world began."*

Science also backs up the truth of eternity. Thermodynamic Law states that energy cannot be created or destroyed. It can only change its form. We are energy, meaning that we will be transformed at death into another energy force. My research shows that science reinforces the concept of creation. After researching the matter from a logical, objective standpoint, I have seen enough to say that creation by God is a certain and absolute truth. The only God whose every word comes true is the God of the Old Testament and the New Testament. The Bible has close to two thousand prophecies. Jesus fulfilled over three hundred prophecies.

The Bible uses symbolism quite often and needs to be interpreted. At other times, we can take it literally. Here are more Bible verses about life after death and how we all live forever:

> *"Behold, I shew you a mystery; we shall not all sleep, but we shall all be changed. The dead shall be raised incorruptible, and we shall be changed. This mortal must put on immortality" (1 Cor. 15:51-53).*

Chapter 10

Coincidence

When we begin a personal relationship with God, we become aware of coincidences. As Christians we realize this is a method God uses to operate in our lives. During my journey, I was always watchful and aware of the possibilities, always open to change and to following God's will.

At this time, I am a successful landlord and sheet metal worker. As I wait for God's direction, I take courses relating to God's Word. I met a minister who taught classes in downtown Barrie, Ontario. I got to wondering about my future in construction and being a landlord. I enjoy both, and I do not want to lose the security they provide. This minister told me one day during his class that the Holy Spirit was indicating to him that I should sell one of my rental houses, which I lived in as well. I took that to heart. I believe that when God wants us to do His will, He will give us confirmation of what He wants.

This confirmation came to me later, when I receive an unsolicited call from a real estate broker. He called out of the blue—by "coincidence." He asked if I was interested in selling my house. I replied that I had been thinking of selling. It turned out that the real estate agent was a born-again Christian whom the Lord had saved from an alcohol addiction. After that confirmation, I was convinced that the Lord wanted me to sell my house. I didn't want to, because the house was beautiful and was generating income.

I decided to quit my well-paying job in the union so I could dedicate my life, full-time, to the Lord. I spent the next few years doing nothing but investigating the truth, finding evidence from all directions, including science, history, and the Holy Bible. It all pointed to one truth. I began studying the Word of God and taking every course I could find. During this time, I also spent about a year renovating my other house to move into. I built a home church, and I look to expanding the church during these end times.

Another interesting coincidence came when I was on the phone with my union. I was calling to quit the union and take out my pension. Right at the moment I called and the person answered, a song by Tom Petty came on. The song was "Jammin Me," and the lyrics that came up right at that instant were: "Take back that pension plan." Again, it was a small coincidence, and I felt that God was just letting me know I was on the right track.

During my period of education and testing after I was saved by Jesus, I had a miracle of God happen to me. I was at the beach with my wife and daughter, where we sat in the water and played. I was well-attuned to my surroundings, as I am always ready to do God's will. I noticed a young, attractive woman sitting on the beach. I could see that she was depressed and upset about something. My heart goes out to all my brothers and sisters in the world, and I want nothing more than to help people. So I was unnerved by this woman's sorrow.

I pointed this out to my wife. I said to her, "If I get a sign from God to talk to this woman, I will go and talk to her and see if I can help change her mood." Minutes later, as we were watching her, we saw two young twin girls, approximately eight to ten years old, stop at the depressed woman, split up, and walk around her. That was totally weird, so I decided it was a sign from God.

Next, I needed to find a way to talk to the woman without seeming abrupt. As perfect timing would have it, my daughter said she wanted to leave. This gave me perfect timing, and I mustered the courage to talk to a total stranger. As we left, I stopped and crouched down next to the lady and said, "Are you okay?" She commented that she was okay. She reassured me that she was fine, and that was the end of our conversation. After we left her, we looked back and saw that she looked happy and was listening to music. By showing the woman that a stranger cared about her, I had changed her attitude completely. I have no doubt that God was directing me to this woman. I get emotional every time I relate this story, because it proves to me that God is working in my life. Being able to help people is the greatest gift. Truly, giving is better than receiving.

Another great miracle of God in my life was when I was engaged to be married. I wanted God's blessing for my marriage. We were at our church, speaking with our minister about our marriage plans. I asked him if we could pray for a sign from God that He would bless this marriage and that it was His will. So we prayed to the Lord, asking Him to give us a sign. At that point in our walk with God, we fully expected a response because of the intensity of our experiences.

Sure enough, the Lord answered us with these "coincidences." We saw three wedding in two days. The first was in a local park. The next day we went to see some relatives in Northern Ontario. In the middle of nowhere in cottage country, we saw a wedding party. Later that day, we drove through a small Ontario town and saw the third wedding on a large ferry boat.

I met a nice, older lady at the church I attended. I gave her a ride home after church one day and asked her when and where she had been saved. She answered, "Peel Street." I was amazed, because Jesus had saved me when I lived on Peel Street too. I also found it noteworthy that we had both been saved on a street named "Peel," as being saved was like having the bad layers peeled away from our souls. Again, it was not a coincidence but God's nudging us, saying, *I am working in your lives.*

A miracle is just an act of God. Any small interaction can be considered a miracle. We all have to start giving glory to God when we have a coincidence. Remember my saying: "If it's a coincidence, then that is a coincidence." These so called coincidences are most often God working in our lives. Let's take heed and pay attention to God's miracles, big or small. They sometimes come in the form of coincidences. After some dedication to the Lord, a good servant should expect some of the greater miracles of healing, visions, guidance, casting out demons, and so on. Jesus spent His time praying and focusing on others. He preached the gospel. He also healed the sick and cast out demons. Jesus spent His time in these ways, so if we are to be disciples of Jesus, we are called to walk with Him.

"Pray one for another, that ye may be healed. The effectual fervent prayer of a righteous man availeth much" (James 5:16).

Chapter 11

Prophetic Words from a Child

At the time I found God in power and truth, I experienced approximately two weeks where I had the Holy Spirit working in me. He showed me incredible wisdom in perfect order. During this awesome period, my daughter Coryn, who was just barely talking at the time, said some prophetic words during playtime. I have to reiterate that she was very young.

As we were playing, Coryn got a Crown Royal purple velvet bag with a few treats in it, some popsicle sticks, and a bowl. She then said, "We must eat Chinese food before we get a bag of trick-or-treats." Unfortunately, the prophecy behind her words is a warning. During the end times, it is quite possible that full-out nuclear war could happen, and the Chinese have the manpower to take over power. I'm not saying that this is a guaranteed prophecy, but it is a possibility. My interpretation of the bag of trick-or-treats is that, at the end, we all get heaven (treats) or hell (tricks). Either way, the Devil, the Antichrist, and the New World Order are positioned to take full control of this world. Jesus is our only protection and the gateway to eternal love, peace, joy, and contentment.

Chapter 12

How to Find God and Increase His Power in Your Life

"If any of you lack wisdom, let him ask of God, that giveth to all men liberally, and upbraideth not [without criticism]; and it shall be given to them" (James 1:5).

The best way to find God and build a relationship with Him is to pray with all your heart. Fasting and denying your pleasures is a great way to show God you are serious about Him.

After Jesus was baptized, He began His ministry to the world. He went straight to battle with the Devil. Jesus fasted for forty days and forty nights. He was also tempted by the Devil. This can be a typical experience for a born-again Christian. When we give our lives to Jesus, the Devil will try to get us back on the dark side of sin. We go through trials and tribulations. This way God purifies us, and our true hearts are shown to God. Fasting may bring our sins to the surface so they can be identified, and healing can occur. Fasting shows the Lord that we are serious. If our desire to eat is greater than our desire to serve God, then the Devil has a foothold in our lives.

I went though salvation, wisdom, and testing—in that order. As soon as I was saved, I was given wisdom, and then I was tested by God. I was shown to fast and to deny the Devil, and I was victorious.

Jesus said that when we fast, we are to do it in private and not make a big deal about it to the world. God sees what we do in private and promises to reward us openly for fasting properly without complaining and making a show of it to others *(Matt. 6:16-18)*.

Fasting may reveal things that control us. It can be used by God as a testing and healing ground. We may have hidden, unknown sins, and fasting may open the door to healing. Fasting brings us closer to God. It can also enable visions and revelations from God. Fasting cleanses the mind, body, and spirit and acts as a detoxifier for physical health as well. If you choose to fast, make sure you research the topic thoroughly before proceeding.

Even when casting out demons (exorcism), fasting is sometimes needed. The disciples asked Jesus why they couldn't cast out this one particular demon. Jesus said that some situations required fasting and prayer.

> *"This kind can come forth by nothing but prayer and fasting" (Mark 9:29).*

Be obedient to the Word of God. Obey the Ten Commandments. Find a church in which to fellowship with like-minded Christians. We are called to fellowship by the Lord.

> *"Not forsaking the assembling of ourselves to- gether, as the manner of some is; but exhorting*

one another; and so much the more, as ye see the day approaching" (Heb. 10:25).

Here we see that it is important to help, worship, and pray together—even more as the end times approach.

God wants us to seek Him and His truth. He has given us creation, and everything He created gives us evidence of an intelligent Creator.

"And the firmament sheweth his handy work" (Ps. 19:1).

"For the invisible things of him from the creation of the world are clearly seen, being understood by the things that are made, even his eternal power and Godhead, so that they are without excuse" (Rom. 1:20).

This shows that God will not forgive a nonbeliever, because there is evidence all around of a supernatural power at work.

Searching for the Lord may not be easy. We also have an adversary that is evil and unrelenting. Satan will use all his power to stop us from learning the truth. Satan wants to deceive and capture souls from God. One of my favorite Scriptures relates to searching for truth in a world of lies.

"It is the glory of God to conceal a thing: but the honor of kings is to search out a matter" (Prov. 25:2).

This shows that God hides information and truth, and He expects us to search, study, and meditate on the Word to find the answers. We must diligently search with all our hearts.

To know God, one should look at His most important commandments.

> *"And thou shalt love the Lord thy God with all thy heart, and with all thy soul, and with all thy mind, and with all thy strength: this is the first commandment. And the second is like, namely this, Thou shalt love thy neighbor as thyself. There is none other commandment greater than these" (Mark 12:30-31).*

When we follow these commands, God will show us His will. When we walk in the spirit of love and obedience with Jesus, He will show us the way. It is not easy, and we will get resistance from the Evil One.

God promises this:

> *"Behold I stand at the door and knock: if any man hear my voice, and open the door, I will come in to him, and will sup with him, and he with Me" (Rev. 3:20).*

> *"Seek and ye shall find, knock, and it shall be opened unto you" (Matt. 7:7).*

Jesus loves us so much that He was brutally sacrificed for us and our sin. He wants a relationship with us. God has done His part. We must do ours and seek out the Creator while we still have time.

It is important also to avoid deadly sins. When we do sin, we must make sure to repent to the Lord, asking forgiveness with all our heart. Having an unforgiving, bitter, hardened heart will lead you to hell.

> *"Forgive and you shall be forgiven"* *(Luke 6:37).*

> *"If ye forgive not men their trespasses, neither will your Father forgive your trespasses"* *(Matt. 6:15).*

Let's look at the seven deadly sins. These are sins that God hates, and it is important to avoid them at all costs to your soul.

> *"These six things doth the Lord hate; yea, seven are an abomination unto Him: a proud look, a lying tongue, and hands that shed innocent blood, a heart that deviseth wicked imaginations, feet that be swift in running to mischief, a false witness that speaketh lies"* *(Prov. 5:16).*

> *"If we confess our sins, He is faithful and just to forgive our sins, and to cleanse us from all unrighteousness"* *(1 John 1:9).*

Once we find salvation, we must work at keeping it. The lukewarm or backsliding Christian is in danger of losing salvation. A positive, loving attitude, humility, a forgiving heart, and prayer will keep a Christian on the narrow path to heaven. There are hard lessons to learn along the way, such as:

> *"Love your enemies, and pray for those that persecute you" (Matt. 5:44).*

Though it is hard to comprehend sometimes, this Scripture is very important.

People who persecute us are typically spiritually impoverished. We should therefore pity them and pray for their souls. No matter what they have done, we must forgive them. If we forgive and pray for them, we are showing the world and the Lord that we are the better persons by showing love and compassion. We must remember that when someone is persecuting us in a negative way, they may be under dark influences, meaning that the Devil and his fallen angels are the ones behind their insulting behavior. We must think of our human enemy and realize that he is being afflicted by evil force. This is why we pray for our enemies.

The following Scripture defines this.

> *"For we wrestle not against flesh and blood, but against principalities, against powers, against rulers of the darkness of this world, against spiritual wickedness in high places" (Eph. 6:12).*

Please forgive and pray for your brothers and sisters. Don't let pride get in the way. Our true enemy is spiritual, not human. The next time someone wrongs you, it may be the result of demonic influence over them. Instead of resorting to retribution or anger, try forgiving and praying for them.

Chapter 13

Salvation

The most important part of life is to attain salvation for yourself. Jesus is the only way to God and eternal heaven. Jesus said,

> *"I am the Way, the Truth, and the Life: no man cometh unto the Father, but by Me"* *(John 14:6).*

> *"For by grace are ye saved though faith; and that not of yourselves: it is a gift from God"* *(Eph. 2:8).*

Have faith in God and He will guide you.

The next step is to follow God's will, which is found in the Word of God. Love. Give. Repent. Be humble. Avoid sin. We are sinful, so we need a solution for the downfall of mankind. Jesus gave Himself to be the perfect sacrifice in order to reconcile us back to the Creator.

> *"He who believes in the Son hath everlasting life: and he that believes not the Son shall not see life; but the wrath of God abideth on him"* *(John 3:36).*

Not only are we to believe, but we are called to action.

"Confess with your mouth the Lord Jesus, and shalt believe in thine heart that God hath raised Him from the dead, thou shalt be saved" (Rom. 10:9).

We should all be activists for our Lord. Jesus died for us, and we should live for Him. If we are to be true disciples of Christ, then we should be able to be a light to others. What is the consequence of just believing without obedience and prayer?

"Every tree that does not bear good fruit will be cut down and thrown into the fire" (Matt. 7:19).

One way to take a stand for your faith is to be baptized in water.

"Baptism doth also now save us . . . by the resurrection of Jesus Christ" (1 Peter 3:21).

"Repent, and be baptized every one of you in the name of Jesus Christ for the remission of sins, and ye shall receive the gift of the Holy Ghost" (Acts 2:38).

"And Jesus, when he was baptized, went up straightway out of the water: and lo, the heavens were opened up to Him, and He saw

the Spirit of God descending like a dove, and lighting upon Him" (Matt. 3:16).

"For John [the Baptist] truly baptized with water; but ye shall be baptized with the Holy Ghost" (Acts 1:5).

When some people get baptized in water, they also get baptized in the Holy Spirit. This happened to Jesus. The apostles did not get the Holy Spirit baptism until Pentecost. Pentecost happened ten days after Jesus ascended to heaven. That was when Jesus sent the Holy Spirit to the world. Jesus said,

"The Comforter, which is the Holy Ghost, whom the Father will send in my Name, He shall teach you all things, and bring all things to your remembrance, whatsoever I have said unto you" (John 14:26).

"And they were all filled with the Holy Ghost" (Acts 2:4).

The difference between the two baptisms is that one is an act of obedience to the Lord. The Holy Ghost baptism is spiritual, and the Holy Ghost descends upon us in power. I was baptized as a baby, which was ineffective. We should be baptized as adults, because it is a declaration of our faith. My experience progressed through searching, salvation, and then the baptism of the Holy Spirit. Then I was baptized in water for the second time as an adult.

> *"I indeed baptize with water unto repentance: but He that cometh after me is mightier than I, whose shoes I am not worthy to bear: He shall baptize you with the Holy Ghost" (Matt. 3:11).*

Jesus said,

> *"Except a man be born of water and of the Spirit: he cannot enter into the kingdom of heaven" (John 3:5).*

If you are unsaved, all you have to do is pray to the Creator. Seek Him with all your heart, and be patient. It can be a simple prayer, like this: "Lord, please show me the truth." Those with deeper knowledge can pray: "I believe that Jesus is the Son of God and that He lived a sinless life. He was sacrificed on the cross for my sins. I believe that Jesus was raised from the dead. I believe in the Father, the Son, and the Holy Spirit as one God. Jesus, I confess my sins and repent. I receive Jesus as my Lord and Savior. I give my life and my will to you. Thank you, Jesus, amen.

Chapter 14

Spiritual Warfare

After my battle with the Devil, I met a man who had a big, white beard. He looked like Santa Claus—or the way we sometimes picture God. I didn't know him at all, but he spoke to me. That day, I was wearing a T-shirt that showed Jesus' arms, with the pierce marks in His hands and blood trickling out. He mentioned in some way that the shirt was too provocative and that I should be more subtle in my expression about God. I was somewhat shocked. I felt that the Lord was expressing to me His displeasure over my wearing of the shirt at that location. I felt upset that I had made a mistake.

I went to my cottage, feeling depressed. When I got there, I felt uneasy. The weather had turned dreary, and there were hundreds of blackbirds in a tree just outside of my property line. I didn't know it at the time, but I think the Devil was stalking me. The Holy Spirit directed me to read Psalm 35. I was feeling very uneasy, but when I read the Psalm, I knew Jesus was there with me. He had given me a Psalm that dealt with spiritual warfare. I wept in thanks to the Lord. I was so fortunate to be blessed with the Lord's guidance, protection, and love. For this reason, Psalm 35 will always be my favorite. Psalms are, in my opinion, the best Scripture for spiritual warfare. Here are some of the most effective, pertaining to spiritual warfare: Psalm 35, 51, 54, 56, 64, 68, 71, 72, and 102.

Another good tactic for spiritual warfare is praising God.

"In everything give thanks: for this is the will of God in Christ Jesus concerning you" *(1 Thess. 5:18).*

When we are feeling depressed about a situation, the best thing to do is to praise God. When we praise Him in a negative situation, we may open up His ability to bless us. We defeat the Devil when we praise God in our suffering. If we remain positive in a negative situation, the Devil has nothing to work with. Knowing that our current situation is temporary, and having faith in God's plan, we can overcome any situation. There is no escape from suffering in this life. It is how we deal with it that is important. If we take a negative approach, we will get a negative result.

God consistently takes my mistakes and turns them into learning experiences. I know that when something awful happens, God is always there to repair the damage, as long as I have the right attitude.

We need to strive to be positive, loving, forgiving, helpful, and always praising God. I say "strive," because even for the ardent Christian, this is a difficult challenge. In a world of evil, it is a constant struggle to remain positive. If we can achieve such obedience to the Lord, the blessings bestowed can be monumental. We will build a better relationship with God. Walking in faith, love, humility, praise, and repentance can unleash God's power in our lives and even make dreams come true. It happened to me, more than I could ever hope for. I can attest that the road is difficult, but in the end, it is worth it. Our trials are often an opportunity for us to grow spiritually and to get closer in our walk with God. Thank you, Jesus.

> *"The suffering of this present time are not worthy to be compared with the glory which shall be revealed in us" (Rom. 8:18).*

Chapter 15

Healing or Curse?

We have many ills and problems in this life, from disease to mental issues. Some illness may be attributed to abuse. Some can be a generational curse. I think it is important to make sure that our minds are running in optimal condition. Many people spend more time on improving *things* than on our best gift: our spiritual connection. It is known that stress can cause illness. We all live with a certain amount of stress. It's how we deal with our adversary that is important. If we are overloaded with work or situational problems, we should simplify and meditate on God and His Word.

If we draw closer to God, we open the door to His awesome power. Life is about building a relationship with our Creator and conquering our demons, with His power. Once we realize this, put our efforts into repentance for our sins, and praise God in all circumstances with dedication and prayerful effort, we have the power of God in our lives to help us and direct us and to reveal His plan for our lives. His plan will be much better than what we could ever imagine for ourselves.

For a healthy mind and body, let's go right to the source of all power: God. First, we can ask God to show us our infirmities and ask Him to heal us. We have to dispel the incorrect teaching of this world that results in unforgiveness, anger, frustration, racism, and sexual sin. This world teaches and promotes such things. If we walk with God, we can defeat our adversary. We must be rid of such negative influences before we can tap into the power of God.

Some of our problems may be from a generational curse. When someone practices sin over and over, it becomes an inequity. Such sins can be passed on from generation to generation. This sin can invoke a familiar spirit—a demon who is familiar with us and our family's sin. This spirit's goal is to keep us in the bondage—mental or physical— that plagues the family. If parents continue to sin, they can actually pass on a familiar spirit and disease.

Here are Scriptures pertaining to the generational curse. If you think you may have a generational curse, repent of your own sin and that of your predecessors.

> *"And also in the inequities of their fathers shall they pine away with them" (Lev. 26:39).*

> *"And confessed their sins, and the inequities of their fathers" (Neh. 9:2).*

> *"If they shall confess their inequity, and the inequity of their fathers, with their trespass which they trespassed against Me, and that also they have walked contrary unto Me. And if their hearts be humbled, and they then ac- cept the punishment of their inequity. Then I will remember my covenant" (Lev. 26:40-42).*

> *"We acknowledge, O Lord, our wickedness, and the inequity of our fathers" (Jer. 14:20).*

Jesus took all of our sins on the cross. Jesus also took all our sickness.

> *"Who Himself bore our sins in His own body on the tree, that we, having died to sins, might live for righteousness . . . by whose stripes you were healed" (1 Peter 2:24).*

> *"But He was wounded for our transgressions, he was bruised for our inequities . . . and with His stripes we are healed" (Isa. 53:5).*

"Stripes" is a reference to Jesus receiving lashes from a whip. Jewish law stated that a person could be given forty lashes. If the executioner went over that number, he was beaten himself, so it was typical for the executioner to stop at thirty-nine.

> *"Forty stripes save one" (2 Cor. 11:14).*

In 2010, the International Classification of Disease changed the categories of diseases from seventeen to thirty-nine. It looks like Jesus took a stripe for every category of disease for mankind. This means that if we look to God in faith, He can heal us of all our infirmities. If you have a disease that has been passed down from generation to generation, it is likely that you have a curse of familiar spirits. First, you have to recognize the pattern, and then you must pray against the demonic forces. Ask God to heal you. No one can discredit the inordinate number of healing miracles that have been reported. How we think and act is more important spiritually than how we feel. As followers of Jesus, we have the power to take back our physical and mental health.

Jesus said,

> *"Behold, I give unto you power to tread on serpents and scorpions, and over all the power of the enemy; and nothing shall by any means hurt you" (Luke 10:19).*

Let us all put our faith in Jesus, that we may be cured of our infirmities, from physical ailments to negative mind-sets.

I believe that many diseases are born of the Devil, and are meant to test and teach us lessons. Also showing us that with faith many diseases can be overcome with the mighty cleansing power of Jesus. Some infirmities may not be healed and we must accept the condition with grace. This is shown with Paul the Apostle when he had an infirmity given to him.

> *"there was given to me a thorn in the flesh, the messenger of Satan to buffet me, lest I should be exalted above measure. For this thing I besought the Lord thrice, that it might depart from me. And He said unto me, My grace is sufficient for thee: for my strength is made perfect in weakness. Most gladly therefore will I rather glory in my infirmities,*

that the power of Christ may rest upon me.
(2 Cor 12:7-9)

We have to determine if the disease can be cured or not. We must first understand how it came to be. Is it self abuse and the consequences thereof? Or perhaps a generational curse. Praying to God should reveal the nature of the disease and if it can be cured. In all circumstances praise God.

Chapter 16

The Meaning of Life

The meaning of life is really quite simple. God made life for His own pleasure, to share His love and creativity with all.

> *"For thou hast created all things, and for thy pleasure they are and were created"* *(Rev. 4:11).*

The other purpose is for us to glorify God. We do this by obedience to His will.

> *"That God in all things may be glorified"* *(1 Peter 4:11).*

We have this life to either accept or deny Jesus, God, and eternal heaven. To deny our Lord and Saviour Jesus is to follow Satan's path to eternal hell. Each of us must decide. We need to search out and follow God, to pray and be obedient to His Word.

> Jesus speaking *"whosoever therefore shall confess me before men, him will I confess also before my Father which is in heaven. But whosoever shall deny me before men, him will I also deny before my Father." (Matt. 10:32-33)*

"In the beginning was the Word, and the Word was with God, and the Word was God" (John 1:1).

"All scripture is given by inspiration of God, and is profitable for doctrine, for reproof, for correction, for instruction in righteousness: that the man of God may be perfect, thoroughly furnished" (2 Tim. 3:16).

The Holy Bible should be studied as the most important book of life. It is a manual on how to succeed in this corrupt world.

Chapter 17

Anagrams and the Secrets They Reveal

During my research, God showed me anagrams. My own anagrams are prophetic. I found that when we make anagrams from names, we sometimes get a factual description of ourselves.

When I do my own name, it shows a sequence of who I was, what I am now, and my future. My old unsaved self was: Chris Deveaux, which equals "Six Crude Have." Christopher Deveaux equals "Super Cervix Hothead." This describes me in my past as an unsaved sinner. I was a fornicator, and I had a temper when confronted.

Now I am Chris George Deveaux, which equals "Vexed, Grouchier, Sage."

> *"And I gave my heart to know wisdom . . . I perceived that this also is vexation of spirit"* *(Eccl. 1:17).*

For those who love wisdom and truth, there is sorrow. I have learned this firsthand. As wisdom grows, so does suffering. This is because we know the horror of hell and the suffering of God for our sakes. We learn how awful sin really is, how the world is deceived and lost.

"For in much wisdom is much grief: and he that increaseth knowledge increaseth sorrow" *(Eccl. 1:18).*

At the moment, I am exactly at this stage. This life is complicated, and sometimes I am confused as to why things are as they are. "Sage" refers to my wisdom, given to me by God Himself though the Holy Spirit.

My full name gives me my final state: Christopher George Deveaux equals "Good, Excretive, Huge Sharper." This indicates that I have progressed through my sinful battles. I have begun to be good and fruitful. *Excretive* means to get rid of waste. I believe that during these times, God will give me the ability to cast out filthy spirits and to heal the sick.

"To have power to heal sicknesses, and to cast out Devils" (Mark 3:15).

I believe that "Huge Sharper" means that I may be used in the end-times battle against evil. There are many references to swords.

"Out of His mouth, goeth a sharp sword" (Rev. 19:15).

"And the remnant were slain with the sword" (Rev. 19:21).

> *"I came not to send peace, but a sword"*
> *(Matt. 10:34).*

It is interesting to note that my name, CHRISTopher GeOrge Deveaux, contains "Christ God" in its spelling order. This is just another verification that Jesus is God and I am just a humble servant. The name was given to me because I have a calling to spread the gospel of Jesus and to warn the nations that judgment approaches.

To prove that this is not a "coincidence," I researched many names from history to see if I could see a pattern of truth. Here are some famous tyrants in history and their anagrams. Interestingly, it is very hard, if not impossible, to find a pleasant anagram for these people.

- *John Forbes Kerry* equals "he's born for jerky." The only others were too vulgar for me to print. He was a member of the Skull and Bones secret society, is a relative of George Bush, and ran against George Bush for president of the United States.
- *Lucifer* equals "if ulcer."
- *George W. Bush* equals "He grew bogus."
- *George Bush* equals "buggers hoe," "bugs go here," and "huge BS ogre."
- *George Herbert Walker Bush* equals "robber hugger wealth reeks" and "huge beserk rebel warthog."
- *Saddam Hussein* equals "dead in US smash," "mud ass in a shed," and "humans sad side."
- *Adolf Hitler* equals "rill of death," "triad of hell," "a dirt of hell," "drill of hate," and "filth ordeal."

- *Barack Hussein Obama* equals "a man hacks our babies" and "I am a bush snake cobra."

Here are some unusual facts about President Obama.

- His code name is "Renegade," which means "traitor, betrayer, rebel, and lawless one" or "forsaking their faith."
- Before Obama was elected, he announced that he stood for biblical marriage. During his term as president, he has changed his mind, and now he backs gay marriage.
- His birth certificate has been proven to be a forgery.
- His armored limo is called the "Beast." The Holy Bible has many verses on the Beast. The limo is eighteen feet long: 6+6+6=18.
- He represented a district in Chicago with the zip code 60606, which equals 666.
- His home address in Kenwood Chicago was 60615= 666 (1+5).
- Obama was elected on November 4, 2008. The next day, the Illinois state lottery numbers for pick three were 666. Illinois is his home state. The pick before and after 666 came up as 779 and 7779. The numbers 7 and 9 represent God, perfection, and completion.

Obama will lead us to suffering and war. Don't blindly follow this evil man. Do research. The answers are shocking. Jesus said,

> *"And if the blind lead the blind, both shall fall into the ditch" (Matt. 15:14).*

Here I see a coincidence for myself. I was born on Sept 7, 1970, or 9/7/70. The last digits in my phone number are 0779. These are just more signs that my mission in life is to serve the Lord.

I got a feeling from the Holy Spirit one day that I should evict all tenants who were late with rent. Two tenants were late, so I evicted them. When I used the anagram to verify these people, one came out as "a comic pervert" and "all in the den of sin." This confirmed to me that I was doing God's will.

So, you can see a pattern here. If you scratch the surface and research, you can find God behind many circumstances.

Chapter 18

Don't Be Scared: Get Prepared

When you follow God, there is no reason to be afraid. You can trust in Him completely. Fear is of the Devil. The Devil knows his future lies in everlasting torment. He is the one who is terrified and wants us to be like him. He wants to ruin our lives and deceive us, all the way down to hell.

> *"For God hath not given us the spirit of fear; but of power, and of love, and of a sound mind [self-control]" (2 Tim. 1:7).*

> *"Satan, who deceives the whole world" (Rev. 12:9).*

So let's not fear evil. Let's get prepared. Spiritual preparation is what is most important. You must first put God above all else. This Scripture defines what to do:

> *"Trust in the Lord with all thine heart; and lean not unto thine own understanding. In all thy ways acknowledge Him, and He shall direct thy paths. Be not wise in thine own eyes: fear the Lord, and depart from evil" (Prov. 3:5-7).*

The next preparation should be for your physical and financial well-being. If you have a good relationship with the Lord, you will be directed. We will still have to suffer through difficult times, but God will fulfill our needs.

Paper investments are a risky place to be. Invest in silver and gold, because paper money is just that: paper. I recommend more than a year's supply of storable food and water. Learn useful skills like gardening.

Look into alternative power supplies. There is a good chance that the electrical grid will fail for an indefinite time. The ways this could happen are numerous—an electromagnetic pulse weapon, solar flares, and so on.

You should look at where you live geographically. During the end times, there will be all sorts of natural disasters. The elite have already bought their gold, stocked their shelves, and moved to the mountains. I believe the coastal areas will be flooded and destroyed.

"The sea and waves roaring" (Luke 21:25).

That's a brief look at how to prepare for the end times. Pray to the Lord always.

"Pray without ceasing" (Luke 5:17).

Chapter 19

The Holy Lunar Tetrad
and Blood Moons

"And the moon became as blood" (Rev. 6:12).

A *lunar tetrad* is four lunar eclipses in a row. A lunar eclipse is also called a "blood moon." These are not too uncommon. Some of these blood moon tetrads land on Jewish holy days. From this point on, I will call them *holy tetrads*. When this happens, something huge always happens in the world that is specific to Israel. What are the odds that four consecutive blood moons would land on Jewish holy days? The odds are mathematically astronomical. And when we consider that a major event occurs every time, the odds are impossible.

Now, get ready for this bombshell: when these holy tetrads occur, major changes happen. Since AD 162, there have been seven holy tetrads, with only one more tetrad to take place in 2014 and 2015. The next holy tetrad to land on the Jewish holidays is not for another five hundred years. The end times are here, and this is the best evidence to prove that major events are going to take place. I substantiated this information with NASA and verified the Jewish holidays.

During all of these holy tetrads, great changes in the world have taken place. In AD 162, there was exile and persecution of the Jewish people. The next three tetrads happened between AD 795 and AD 861, which was when the Islamic conquest occurred. Their goal was to eradicate Judeo-Christian doctrine. The next tetrad happened in AD 1493, when the Jewish people were exiled from Spain. We see that major changes always happen to the Jewish people and their homeland when these holy tetrads occur.

Now we get to our time line. Let's keep in mind that the Jewish people were God's chosen people. Therefore, prophecy is centered around them.

The next two really get interesting. From 1949 to 1950, the holy blood moon tetrad occurred again. That signaled the miracle of Israel being reborn into a nation after two thousand years. The next tetrad happened in 1967 to 1968. During this time, Israel defeated a larger Arab army in only six days. This was when Israel took back control of Jerusalem—perhaps the most holy city in the world.

The next holy tetrad will happen on April 15, 2014; October 8, 2014; April 4, 2015; and September 28, 2015. This is a guarantee that something big is about to happen to Israel and the world. With all the current wars and rumors of wars, it is certain we are in for change. From this research, I believe war will start in the Middle East between Israel and the Arab nations. This will lead to an all-out nuclear world war. This, in turn, will lead to the New World Order, the rise of the Antichrist, and most importantly, the return of Jesus.

These blood moons are signs that are described in the Holy Bible. They are warnings to those who will listen. Take these warnings to heart.

"And God said, Let there be lights in the firmament of the heaven to divide the day from the night; and let them be for signs, and for seasons, and for days and years" (Gen. 1:14).

"And there shall be signs in the sun, and in the moon, and in the stars, and in the earth distress of nations, with perplexity; the sea and the waves roaring" (Luke 21:25).

I would like to point out some other time lines that give evidence that we are in end times.

There are six days of the week, and then we have the Sabbath day of rest. Biblical scholars suggest that Adam and Eve were created around 4000 BC. We then look at the correlation between the two, we see that 4,000 years plus 2,000 years gives us the present day. To the Lord, one day is like a thousand years.

"Be not ignorant of this one thing, that one day is with the Lord as a thousand years and a thousand years as one day" (2 Peter 3:8).

So, after 6,000 years on earth, we are ready for the end of time. The next thousand years is the reign of Christ (rest).

"But they shall be priests of God and of Christ, and shall reign with Him for a thousand years" (Rev. 20:6).

I would like to point out here the deception of the elite. They have lied to us all and have convinced many that the world is millions of years old. There is no evidence whatsoever of "evolution theory." *Nothing* cannot create *something.* Think of how preposterous it is to believe that everything we are and see was created by nothing. Let's use basic logic: either *something* (God) created the universe, or *nothingness* brought life into existence out of nothing.

Let's look at some amazing facts about things we know but can't feel or see. The earth revolves at over 1,000 miles per hour. The earth is also orbiting the sun at approximately 67,000 miles per hour. Besides that, our whole solar system is traveling at 420,000 to 550,000 miles per hour around the galactic core. We don't see or feel the phenomenal speed. This is clearly the work of an omnipotent God.

> *"For the invisible things of Him from the creation of the world are clearly seen, being understood by the things that are made, even His eternal power and Godhead; so that they are without excuse" (Rom. 1:20).*

This verse says that creation is evidence of God. There will be no excuse for anyone who denies the truth of an all-powerful God.

Jesus told the parable of the fig tree, which is more evidence that we are in the end times. Symbolism is used extensively in the Bible, and in this parable, the fig tree represents Israel.

Jesus said,

> *"Now learn a parable of the fig tree; when her branch is yet tender, and putteth forth leaves, ye know that summer is near: when ye shall see these things come to pass, know that it is nigh, even at the doors. Verily I say unto you, that this generation shall not pass, till all these things be done" (Mark 13:28-30).*

Jesus was saying that when Israel was born (a tender branch), a generation would not pass before the end times would occur. A generation is seventy years, and the birth of Israel took place in 1948. That gives us 2018 as the latest time for the end.

> *"The days of our years are threescore years and ten" (Ps. 90:10).*

A score of years is twenty years.

Chapter 20

The Roman Catholic Church and the Prophecy of the Popes

Some more evidence of the end times is in the "Prophecy of the Popes."

In 1139, Saint Malachy, an Irish archbishop, was on his way to Rome, when he had a vision. He was able to see every pope until the end times. He used cryptic Latin phrases to describe these popes. Our current pope Francis is the last one on the list. Malachy's final words on the last pope are: "Who will feed his flock many tribulations; after which the seven-hilled city [Rome is on seven hills and is the seat of the Roman Catholic Church] will be destroyed, and the dreadful judge will judge the people."

"The seven heads are seven mountains, on which the woman sitteth" (Rev. 16:9).

"The woman" in this verse symbolizes a church. I would like to point out here that the Roman Catholic Church is guilty of many sins. They are responsible for millions of murders throughout their history. They outlawed the Holy Bible and murdered those who had them in their homes. This happened during the Middle Ages.

Here are some major offences of the Catholic Church.

They call their priests "father." This is clearly wrong, for Jesus said,

> *"And call no man your father upon the earth:*
> *for one is your Father, which is in heaven"*
> *(Matt. 23:9).*

Also, no one can absolve sin except God. The Roman Catholic Church is guilty of letting their priests absolve sin. Only Jesus does that. Even the Pharisees of Jesus' time knew the law:

> *"Who can forgive sins but God only?"*
> *(Mark 2:7).*

They also make claims that priests should be celibate. That is not biblical.

They pray to saints, which is forbidden. Angels are fellow servants of the Lord and should not be worshipped.

> *"I fell down to worship before the feet of the*
> *angel. Then saith he unto me, See thou do it*
> *not. For I am thy fellow servant" (Rev. 22:8-9).*

Jesus didn't hold His physical family above anyone else. This is shown in Scripture. When Jesus was teaching, His mother and brother asked to see Him. Jesus went on to teach His group, and He pointed out to them that anyone who follows God's will is His brother, sister, and mother. The Roman Catholic Church idolizes Mary, the mother of

God. They always pray and have large statues of Mary. That is nothing more than worshipping idols.

> *"For whosoever shall do the will of God, the same is my brother, and my sister, and mother" (Mark 3:32-35).*

In AD 380 Roman Emperor Constantine made Christianity the law. Then the Romans joined Christian doctrine with pagan rituals. The Romans who crucified Jesus are now joined together with the church. In the Middle Ages, the Roman Catholic Church was responsible for millions of murders for their "cause."

They currently have their own kingdom called the Vatican. The Lateran Treaty of 1929 was signed by the tyrant Mussolini and the Catholic Church. This gives the Vatican sovereign status as an independent state within Rome. Since the creation of the Vatican, the popes are now called kings, according to the Bible, because they rule a kingdom. To add credence to the Malachy prophecy of the popes, we have this Scripture.

> *"And there are seven kings: five are fallen, and one is, and the other has not yet come; and when he cometh, he must continue a short space. And the beast that was, and is not, even he is the eighth, and is of the seven, and goeth into perdition" (Rev. 17:10).*

This shows that from the birth of the Vatican's kingdom in 1929, there will be seven popes until the end times. It even includes Pope Benedict's reign, describing his reign as a "short space." Almost all popes hold their position until death. The last time a pope abdicated his throne was over six hundred years ago. It is an interesting "coincidence" that the day that Pope Benedict announced his resignation, the Vatican was hit by lightning. We are currently at the last pope. End times are upon us.

The opulence of the Catholic Church is deplorable.

> *"How much she hath glorified herself, and lived deliciously" (Rev. 18:7).*

> *"And the woman [Catholic church] was arrayed in purple and scarlet color and decked with gold, and precious stones, and pearls, having a golden cup in her hand" (Rev. 17:4, 16).*

Here the Bible speaks of the Catholic Church as rich, powerful, and corrupt. Cardinals wear scarlet attire, and the archbishops wear purple robes. They use golden cups with precious stones.

The Vatican has built a telescope in Arizona. They have built it on Apache holy land and have named it *Lucifer.* The Catholic Church has even mentioned that they would "baptize" an alien if they chose to. The Catholic Church will play a large role in end-times deception. They will say that the aliens are not a threat. I believe that the Catholic

Church may provide the "false prophet," as written about in Revelation. If you are a Catholic, I ask you to research this so you are not deceived.

God will not keep those who love Him in ignorance. God sends His prophets out into the world to warn the people of their coming destruction.

> *"The Lord God will do nothing, but he revealeth his secret unto his servants the prophets" (Amos 3:7).*

God is good, fair, and just. He will give us fair warning when destruction approaches. Listen to the prophets who are warning the world now of impending danger. The message is warning of destruction, and the solution is to pray and repent. We cannot stop what is written about the end times. We can only put our faith and love in God. Only He can deliver and protect us from the evil that's spreading over this world.

Chapter 21

Revelation and End Times

"Blessed is he that readeth, and they that hear the words of this prophecy, and keep those things which are written therein: for the time is at hand" (Rev. 1:3).

During these end times, the last book of the Bible becomes the most important Scripture. Revelation gives us the details of what will happen during these incredible times.

"The revelation of Jesus Christ, which God gave unto Him, to shew unto his servants things which must shortly come to pass" (Rev. 1:1).

Revelation shows the time line of destruction that will soon descend upon the earth. Chapter 6 describes the opening of the seven seals. This is the beginning of the end.

The first seal to be opened unleashes the "white horse." This symbolizes a leader who is given power to conquer. The second seal reveals a "red horse," which signifies that power is given to a leader to "take peace from the earth." Next, a "black horse" describes economic collapse. The "pale horse" is next, and on this horse rides death, with hell following. Power is given to the rider to kill one quarter of the earth.

The sixth seal brings natural disasters. There will be a great earthquake, the sun will be darkened, and the moon will become blood-red. The stars of heaven will fall onto the earth. This likely indicates that meteors will fall, causing great destruction. The Bible also states that every mountain and island will be moved out of its place. This could refer to a pole shift, which would be devastating. Science has proved that the North Pole is already shifting. In Florida, they had to repaint all of the runway markers to correspond to the new pole location.

The next seal initiates a stage in which seven trumpets usher in even more suffering on earth. The first trumpet brings hail and fire mingled with blood. This could describe smaller, fiery asteroids that hit planes, as this could create such a scenario. A third part of the trees will be destroyed, as will all the green grass.

The second trumpet announces, "As it were, a great mountain burning with fire was cast into the sea, and a third part of the sea became blood." Here, it looks like a giant asteroid hits the ocean. The contamination of the sea could be a result of pollutants that come with the asteroid. A third of the sea life and ships will be destroyed.

The third trumpet is similar, as a great, burning star called "Wormwood" will fall upon the waters. A third of the water on earth will become poisonous, and many people will die from drinking this bitter water.

The fourth trumpet darkens the sun, moon, and stars. The fifth trumpet unleashes demonic beings that will attack and sting the unholy like scorpions. The sixth trumpet sets loose four demons into the world to kill a third of mankind.

After the seventh trumpet sounds, Jesus will return and separate the saved from the unsaved. This is a brief look at the time line of the book of Revelation.

It is not difficult to look around and see the degradation as this world descends into sin.

> *"In the last days, perilous times shall come. For men will be lovers of their own selves, covetous, boasters, proud, blasphemers, disobedient to parents, unthankful, unholy, without natural affection, truce-breakers, false accusers, fierce, despisers of those that are good, lovers of pleasures more than lovers of God" (2 Tim. 3:1-4).*

Just look at history to see what we have done. We have outlawed prayer in schools. Same-sex marriage is spreading, which is an abomination in God's sight. Sex before marriage is more common than waiting. Glorification of violence and sex in society though movies and TV. Pornography is a booming business. New-age spiritualism is rising, because people want to believe in God, but they want to make up their own rules to suit their desires. We live in a time of war, and there are many rumors of war. Earthquakes are increasing in magnitude and frequency, and they are happening all over the world.

> *"Ye shall hear of wars and rumors of wars . . . and earthquakes in diverse places" (Matt. 24:6-7).*

Many Scriptures written a long time ago could not be interpreted until today.

> *"O Daniel, shut up the words, and seal the book, even to the time of the end: many shall run to and fro, and knowledge shall be increased . . . for the words are closed up and sealed till the time of the end" (Dan. 12:4, 9).*

"Many shall run to and fro" is a reference to our modern transportation. We are now living in the information age. The world's knowledge is available in seconds with computers. It is estimated that, from Jesus' time to 1900, our knowledge doubled. From 1900 to 1950, it is said to have doubled again. By the 1960s, knowledge was doubling every two years.

In the last part of the verse in Daniel it says *"the words are closed up and sealed till the end of time"*. This refers to some Bible prophecies not being understood when they were written. Only those in the end times will be capable of deciphering some prophecies. An example of this is the parable of the fig tree (Mark 13: 28-30) giving a time-line of 70 years from the birth of Israel in 1948,, to the end times. Another Bible prophecy that wouldn't be understood until end times is

> *"there flesh shall consume away while they stand upon their feet, and their eyes shall consume away in their holes, and their tongue shall consume away in their mouth."*
> *(Zech 14:12)*

This is a warning to the people who attack and want the destruction of Jerusalem. This prophecy relates to the use of thermonuclear weapons. Only now do we have the technology to melt and kill the body instantly where it stands. The temperature of a nuclear bomb is millions of degrees. Nuclear destruction may be used to bring about the fall of Damascus as prophesied in Isaiah.

> *"Damascus is taken away from being a city,*
> *and it shall be a ruinous heap." (Isaiah 17:1)*

Damascus is the oldest city in the world never to be destroyed or left in a ruinous heap. Syria is a terrorist stronghold and many have anti-Semitic. views They are currently in civil war. My interpretation that Israel will strike Damascus with nuclear weapons in the near future, especially as the Holy Lunar Tetrad approaches in 2014. In 2007 Israel threatened to wipe Syria off the map is they attacked with chemical weapons. Currently Israel is also threatening Iran with a possible nuclear strike if Iran continues their nuclear program. With Russia and China as allies, Iran could be a catalyst for world war 3.

We can even see redundancy in movies and music. Movies dealing with end times destruction and alien invasions are common, Mainstream pop music is full of evil imagery and demonic symbolism. Sports is just a business now, and it is all about money. The purity is long gone in these areas. No matter where you look, the signs of the end times are here.

Chapter 22

Finally, the Good News

With all that apocalyptic doom on the horizon, it's nice to know that it ends well for all who love God and do His will. Jesus will return in power to destroy His enemies. He came first as a servant, the perfect sacrificial Lamb. Now He will return with justice and punishment for the evil ones and with reward for His faithful servants. He will separate the good from the evil, wheat from tares, sheep from goats.

> *"Gather ye together first the tares, and bind them in bundles to burn them: but gather the wheat into My barn" (Matt. 13:30).*

> *"Before Him shall be gathered all nations: and He shall separate them one from another, as a shepherd divideth his sheep from the goats" (Matt. 25:32).*

> *"Behold, He cometh with clouds" (Rev. 1:7).*

> *"Behold, I come as a thief. Blessed is he that watcheth" (Rev. 16:15).*

> *"There shall be no more death, neither sorrow, nor crying, neither shall there be any more pain" (Rev. 21:4).*

"Behold, I come quickly, and My reward is with Me, to give every man according as his work shall be" (Rev. 22:12).

For Christians, this is a time to get closer to God. For agnostics and atheists, it is their last chance to find the truth and salvation. May God be with you.

Chapter 23

The Last Chapter, in More Ways Than One

In this book, I hope I have provoked the reader to investigate and research the intricate web of deceit that rules our everyday life. I could only scratch the surface of these topics. I encourage the reader to delve in, to get all the facts.

The NWO has despicable plans for the world. May you all prepare yourselves spiritually and physically.

More importantly, I hope to have inspired the reader to get closer to our Lord and Savior. I wrote this book out of love for my fellow brothers and sisters. My calling is to serve God. By the providence of our Lord, may Jesus use my book to save souls.

Jesus said,

> *"Let the light shine before men, that they may see your good works, and glorify your Father, which is in heaven" (Matt. 5:16).*

To God be the glory. I hope to see you in heaven!